THROUGH A MIRROR DIMLY: THE EPISCOPAL CHURCH'S
NATIONAL COMMISSIONS FOR WORK AMONG THE BLACKS, 1865 – 1904

David F. O. Thompson

Submitted in partial fulfillment
of the requirements for the
Degree of Master of Sacred Theology
in the General Theological Seminary
New York City.

15 April 1985

TABLE OF CONTENTS

Black Freedom and White Fear

The Rev. John F. W. Ware preached a sermon at the First Independent Church in Baltimore, Maryland on 5 February 1865. It was just two short months before the Civil War was to end, and this preacher and his parishioners were aware of the war's approaching demise. Thoughts of peace both comforted and frightened them because they were concerned about the changes it would bring, especially in regard to the freeing of the slaves. They knew how to treat slaves, but they were not sure how to react to the freeing of slaves. One thing was certain, freed blacks were not their equal, no matter what the law said. They could not be because the black race was ignorant and devoid of civilized instinct and manners. Only through education could the black population ever become equal to the white. Mr. Ware said:

> The edict of the State has set free the slave.
> The slave is a dangerous element, as a slave,
> before, is a more dangerous element as a free man
> now. Why? He is without wanted restraint. He is
> ignorant, he may become a vagabond, and then
> vicious, and then--why, danger--new laws, new
> jails, new police, the cumbersome, costly,
> superficial, tawdry uncertain cure. It all lies
> in a nutshell today. You will have the scum of
> slaves upon you. They must be met by prisons and
> punishments, or by education.... [1]

It is hard to explain or even understand this great trepidation upon the part of the whites who dreaded the release of the black people from their slavery. They were

convinced that the black people were not civilized and had to be controlled by the superior, white race for the good of all American citizens. The freeing of the slaves meant that the whites no longer had direct, physical control over the blacks. This made the whites fearful and uncertain about the future of the country, and consequently, they developed both laws and mores which would ensure that the blacks were enslaved by a new, insidious slavery: racial prejudice.

Slavery itself had been firmly established by 1660 in the American colonies and was regarded as an institution by 1700. [2] Slaves had no rights, no personal freedoms; they were owned by a white "master" who had total control over their lives. Whites assumed, from their earliest contacts with the blacks, that they were an inferior race. Blacks were not "real" humans; they were caricatures, barbarians, a Godly mistake. They certainly were not white, or cultured or civilized and therefore were not fully human; perhaps, half human and half animal, but not fully human. They were "things," one step below a human. Jordan Winthrop writes:

> Englishmen did not enslave one another. As we
> have seen, however, Englishmen did possess a
> concept of slavery, formed by the clustering of
> several rough but not illogical equations. The
> slave was treated like a beast. Slavery was
> inseparable from the evil in men; it was God's
> punishment upon Ham's prurient disobedience.
> Enslavement was captivity, the loser's lot in a
> contest of power. Slaves were infidels or
> heathens. [3]

Like animals and livestock, the whites came to believe they

had the right to capture them, sell them, and enslave them. The black race was dehumanized by the whites who turned them into a commodity for the white world's profit.

But the blacks were human, and beneath the indignities, beneath the toil and strife were human beings who yearned to be free and to have the same rights and responsibilities as the white people. Some whites sensed that the blacks were more human than society wanted to admit, and these whites attempted to lessen the oppression that the blacks experienced by trying to humanize their working and living conditions and by bringing them spiritual salvation, so they would be able to experience God's freedom in the next world. No matter how many freedoms the blacks would win, they would always be bound by chains of racism, which resided side by side with slavery. However, few religious institutions spoke against slavery and racism. This was especially true of the Episcopal Church, which typically accepted slavery and racism as facts of life.

This approval can be seen in the sermon delivered in the congregation of Christ Church in Hartford, Connecticut in 1850. The Rev. Dr. Wheaton preached on St. Paul's Epistle to Philemon and talked about the duty of northern citizens in regard to slavery. He argued:

> The repugnance remains, unconquered and uncon-
> querable; and the inferior race must, by a law
> which we cannot control, remain under some kind of
> subordination to the higher intellect of the
> Anglo-Saxon, till it shall please God to lift up
> the curse, pronounced four thousand and five

hundred years ago..... As Joseph's brethern, when
they sold him into Egypt, meant it for evil, and
God meant it for good; so may blessings
incalculable yet spring from an act, evil in
itself--the carrying away of the African, to
sojourn for a time in a state of bondage. [4]

This excerpt contains all the stereotypes of the black
race as perpetuated in the general society. The preacher did
not use his understanding of the Bible to question society's
myths but rather used his Biblical knowledge to convince
himself and others that blacks were not equal to whites. His
thinking was very typical, although some clergy and laity
would have disagreed. The Church was sure that slavery was
justified because blacks were inferior and consequently
benefited from their contacts with the white race.
Furthermore, the Bible justified such conclusions because it
did not condemn slavery. Even those who believed slavery was
evil were convinced that it was sanctioned by New Testament
teachings. Certainly the religious leaders of the day could
not condemn that which was tolerated by the Apostles! One
minister wrote:

The New Testament nevertheless no more requires us
to look upon a Slaveholder, than it does upon a
soldier, as a criminal. While giving the
institution then no positive sanction, it
tolerates the relationship between master and
slave.... We believe all the South asks at our
hands, is our toleration of what the New Testament
tolerates beyond the possibilities of a doubt....
[5]

John Henry Hopkins, Episcopal Bishop of Vermont,

insisted in 1864, after the issuance of the Emancipation Proclamation, that slavery was accepted by the Old and New Testaments. He proposed that St. Paul did not speak against slavery because he "knew the will of the Lord Jesus Christ, and was only intent in obeying it." This very basic conclusion led to other conclusions just as detrimental to the black population: the Bible was the highest source of knowledge in the world and could not be questioned or tampered with, not even in light of new understandings or teachings. [6] This radical fundamentalism did not permit new perceptions to emerge in regard to slavery. Fortunately, Bishop Hopkins' thoughts were not accepted by the entire Episcopal Church, and concerned Episcopalians issued pamphlets refuting his thesis, yet his arguments highlight the common belief that was held by the Episcopal Church for many years. The Church rethought this issue when forced to by events in the secular society: the emancipation of the slaves in 1863 and the defeat of the Confederate States in 1865. After all, it could not justify slavery when the United States Government declared it to be illegal. The lead of society was followed and the Church accepted the end of slavery when society deemed slavery to be evil.

The Episcopal Church so easily embraced slavery because it was the successor of the Church of England whose role in society was both to Christianize and to pacify the American colonies. Therefore, the Church of England brought to the

American shores the Christian Gospel and the English culture. Gospel and culture were intertwined, inseparable because the Church was an official government organization. It could not escape from this dual role of serving both heavenly and earthly kings. Therein lay the problem. The Gospel had to be interpreted to accept the traditional English values, beliefs, and mores. One could not expect the Church of England minister to protest very often against the government and have him retain his position or his head! Since the government and culture accepted slavery under British rule, the Episcopal Church did not question this institution once it became independent from the Church of England following the Revolutionary War. It could not question what it did not see!

In this paper I want to look at how the Church dealt with the freeing of the slaves and scrutinize the work of two Episcopal Church commissions that dealt with the freed blacks: The Home Missions Commission for Colored People, 1865-1877 and the Commission for Work among Colored People, 1887-1904. These commissions were predominately white groups which were established by the Episcopal Church to aid it in ministering to the needs and concerns of the black people. The General Convention hoped that these agencies would help the black people adjust to their newly won freedom and also enable the Church to win new converts. These goals were only partially achieved because Church members could not accept

the idea that the black race was equal to the white race. Always, the black people were seen as outsiders with a different culture and identity.

In spite of the Church officials' resolve to serve the black race, the Episcopal Church membership did not enthusiastically support the black missionary projects and the Church's theological and organizational structure was not flexible enough to serve the black needs. The Church's demand for ordered services and educated clergy, and its inability to recognize its own prejudicial attitudes prevented the missionaries from reaching large numbers of black people. Church officials were aware that something was not quite right in the way they conducted their missionary programs, but they could never agree as to what was wrong. The aforementioned commissions, which will be discussed at length later, were condemned to dwell in a twilight zone; success was before their eyes as failure nipped at their heels. The Episcopal Church, the Church of Apostles and Martyrs did not know how to deal with this strange race of black people suddenly freed from centuries of bondage. Neither did the country. The Church mirrored the perplexity felt by many white people: How was the United States to deal with the black race as a freed people? The answer to this disturbing question was not readily found, but neither was the decision to release the slaves from bondage easily made. Intellectual debates about slavery pitted friend against

friend and state against state. The brutality of slavery was to be ended, ironically, only through more brutality and bloodshed.

The tension that surrounded the peculiar institution of the South finally forced the nation to go to war against itself. This war was not really about the rights of blacks but was a contest of strength: which was stronger, the federal government or the individual states which declared that if they did not like the federal policy they could break away? Certainly the war swirled around the issues that arose because of slavery but it was not necessarily a war to end human bondage and to gain rights for the black people. This was dramatically portrayed when President Lincoln at first refused to allow free, black men to be inducted into the armed forces. He like many other whites believed the blacks did not have the intelligence or the conviction to fight for the country. The Union navy did use former Confederate slaves who were declared to be "contraband" to serve as "apprentice seamen and the Army began to employ them extensively as laborers and officer's servants." [7] Finally Congress passed legislation in 1863 allowing black men to join the forces in order to bolster the Union forces because of the great number of casualties and the unexpectedly long, length of the war. [8]

The President's reluctance to allow the blacks to join the armed services foreshadowed their lack of acceptance by

their white colleagues and indeed by their white enemy. The black soldiers were second-class citizens who did not receive the same promotions, pay, or benefits for dependents that the white soldiers received. [9] This demeaning situation was supported by the officers of the Union forces and by President Lincoln. They believed it would be too degrading for the white soldiers to have to fight along side the blacks and receive the same level of pay. It was also thought that the blacks should be willing to make such sacrifices because they were fighting for their own freedom and had more to gain than did the whites who already had freedom. [10] To add to this indignity was the deadly reality that Confederate troops made little effort to allow black Union soldiers to become prisoners of war; they would rather kill them. At least 300 black soldiers were massacred by Confederate troops after the blacks had laid down their arms and had surrendered at Fort Pillow, Tennessee on 12 April 1864. [11] Such atrocities only made the black soldiers more determined to win the war, and some units became renowned for their ferociousness, since they knew many Confederate soldiers would not allow them to surrender. When black soldiers were taken as prisoners, the white Confederate population looked upon the sight of black soldiers as extremely odious, and a Richmond paper stated the blacks should be separated from the white soldiers and placed "'into a pen' until their status was determined and their owners located." [12] Whether blacks lived in the North or

South, they discovered that their freedom was defined not by laws but by the whims of the white population.

The Civil War ended on 9 April 1865. [13] The war for black freedom did not end on this date but was carried on by the black people in each state and territory. This time the war was not fought with guns and ammunition but with words, actions, and attitudes. The slaves who were told of their freedom were ecstatic. They could hardly believe that they now had the right to control the daily activities of their lives. The feelings of one black slave, Aunt Sissy, highlights the deep and profound exhilaration that all the former slaves felt. She said: "'Isn't I a free woman now! De Lord can make Heaven out of Hell any time, I do believe.'" [14] Many of the freed slaves left their old masters and became associated with new plantations. Their life did not change all that much but their moving to a new home and plantation demonstrated their newly granted freedom. Some also publicly announced their surnames, surnames they either just adopted or had secretly hidden from their masters. Obtaining a new home, a new job, and a surname enabled the former slave to realize that he did indeed have more freedom that he had before as a slave.

Some former slaves did not know that they had gained liberation from their masters until Union troops came to their area of the country, and some had to wait until an official of the newly formed Freedmen's Bureau told them of

their liberty months after the fact. This new liberty did not guarantee better living conditions, and some aspects of their life became worse because, as Leon Litwack points out, the whites realized that this former investment and commodity was now a financial loss. Furthermore, the former white masters lived and worked with the slaves day after day in a purgatory-type existence, with the slaves' very presence reminding them of how much pride, honor, and money they had lost with the coming of the slaves' freedom. The whites would just as soon kill the blacks as to look at them. [15] The old way of life was dead, and the whites were forced to accept that fact, but they were not forced to accept the black race into their new, post-slavery world.

The federal government feared that the reunion of the country was to be an arduous task. Congress established the Bureau of Refugees, Freedmen and Abandoned Land in order to aid the freedmen. [16] This bureau faced a monumental task. The South had been devastated by the war, and the white population was reluctant to grant any concessions to the blacks. The blacks felt that they had a right to land in order to start a new life, but the federal and state governments refused to take such a radical step as distributing land to this newly freed population. The Freedmen's Bureau acted more like a buffer between the two conflicting sides than as dynamic force in changing the plight of the black people. But this in itself must be seen

as a victory, for the whites were intent in driving the blacks back into slavery, even if it had to be called by a new name. The House of Representatives asked that a report be presented in regard to the status of the states that were "lately in rebellion." Major General Carl Schurz reported the following to the House on 12 December 1865:

> Aside from the assumption that the negro will not work without physical compulsion, there appears to be another popular notion prevalent in the south, which stands as no less serious an obstacle in the way of a successful solution of the problem. It is that the negro exists for the special object of raising cotton, rice and sugar for the whites, and that it is illegitimate for him to indulge like other people, in the pursuit of his own happiness in his own way....
> But while accepting the 'abolition of slavery,' they think that some species of serfdom, peonage, or some other form of compulsory labor is not slavery, and may be introduced without a violation of their pledge. Although formally admitting negro testimony, they think that negro testimony will be taken practically for what they themselves consider its 'worth.' What particular shape the reactionary movement will assume is at present unnecessary to inquire. There are a hundred ways of framing apprenticeship, vagrancy, or contract laws, which will serve the purpose. Even the mere reorganization of the militia upon the old footing will go far towards accomplishing the object.... [17]

Major General Carl Schurz's prophetic and sensitive report did accurately predict what the black population was to face in the days, months, and years following their emancipation. The whites did not want their culture contaminated by the black, African world, so the world of slavery was replaced with enslaving laws and customs. Blacks

were not allowed to use the same public transportation cars as whites, to eat in the same restaurants, to go to the same schools, to use the same parks, or to stay in the same hotels. [18] The white, supreme world was to be enforced at all costs. Whites did not want the two cultures to mix, so distinctions between the two races had to made. Seeking relief and a new future, many blacks flocked to the urban centers hoping to find the freedom promised to them in the constitution. They were mistaken to believe that the urban life was physically or materially much better than the rural. They were forced to live in undesirable areas and forced to work for whatever wages the white world was willing to pay. Their chains of slavery were replaced with the shackles of white prejudice. But in spite of this terrorizing prejudice, blacks had one thing in the urban centers that they did not have out in the isolated rural areas, support; the support of churches, schools, benevolence societies, the Freedmen's Bureau. The oppression could be shared and endured in the urban centers.

Even with the support of their brothers and sisters and liberal whites, the blacks soon came to realize that their world was neither understood or appreciated by the whites. The whites established black schools of learning and administrated aid as much out of fear and pity as they did out of a sense of justice and respect. Many felt that the blacks were a simple, childish race that had to be helped in

order that the country would not be hindered by their great ignorance and superstitious beliefs. They were a burden given to this country by God, and the country had to endure this taxing responsibility. The feeling expressed by this southern man could be found anywhere in the United States:

> 'The different races of man, like different coins at a mint, were stamped at their true value by the Almighty in the beginning. No contact with each other--no amount of legislation or education--can convert the negro into a white man. Until that can be done--until you can take the kinks out of his wool and make his skull thinner-- until all these things and abundantly more have been done, the negro cannot claim equality with the white race.' [19]

It would seem that only God could ease the tension building between the two races. The blacks needed a miracle. What they received instead were Northern organizations who came to the South to help them gain respect and dignity in the white world.

HOME MISSIONS COMMISSION, 1865 - 1877

The Episcopal Church's triennial General Convention met in October 1865 to formulate church legislation and to receive reports from its various committees and commissions. Delegates were grateful that the war was over and made every attempt to ensure that the Episcopal Church remained united. Church divisions which existed during the war were never formally acknowledged by the Church, so no official censure was leveled at those dioceses who were part of the Confederate Episcopal Church. Knowing that the Church had escaped the war with its unity, the General Convention could proceed with God's work.

The delegates knew, as well, that this newly reunited country had changed. The peculiar institution of slavery had been destroyed by the Union's victory, and now they felt compelled to assist the country by helping the freed slaves adjust to their new liberty. Freedom had been granted, but no one was sure the black race could cope with their new privileges and responsibilities. Many delegates were fearful that the black race might abuse their liberty and fall back into what the whites believed to be superstitious secular and religious behavior: religious fervor without the benefit of an educated, reasonable mind. The General Convention

believed that the Episcopal Church was well suited to provide the blacks with a satisfactory religion because of its emphasis upon a reasoned and orderly worship service. Consequently, one committee warned the General Convention of the arduous task ahead of the Church in helping the blacks adjust to their new secular and religious freedoms:

> It is obvious to every mind that the Domestic field never made such demands upon the zeal and liberality of the Church as now. The termination · of our fearful civil war makes free again the tide of immigration, which will soon spread over all our Western borders; it opens to us a large section of the country desolated by fire and sword, and needing help for the restoration of altars, and the support of its ministers; and it has thrown upon the charity of the church millions of an ignorant and almost helpless race, who are to be taught, and Christianized, and fitted for their new position. [1]

The General Convention of 1865 therefore created the Protestant Episcopal Freedman's Commission, eventually called the Home Missions Commission to Colored People (Home Missions Commission), to educate the blacks. [2] This Commission was part of the Church's Domestic and Foreign Missionary Society and was answerable to the Society's Board of Missions. It was composed of a secretary, general agent, treasurer, and an executive committee, which had power to act for the whole body when the Commission was in recess. [3] Its membership consisted of twenty-eight white men, including bishops, presbyters, and laity. [4]

The General Convention stated that the Home Missions

Commission's objective was the "religious and other instruction of the freedmen." [5] The Commission faithfully followed this objective throughout its history. Indeed, the Commission stated in 1866 that its education would consist of "useful and elementary knowledge, religious and secular" and that any other aid given to the freed blacks should be "subsidiary to the work of education." [6] The Commission never officially defined what form "useful and elementary" education would take. However, an editorial about educating the blacks appeared in Spirit of Missions, in the Freedman's Section. This editorial- "The Freedman's Commission & Questioners" -answered the criticisms and questions that Episcopalians had directed toward the Commission and its work. The editorial said this about educating the freed blacks:

> It is simply its duty [the Commission]--accepting, with thankfulness to God the fact of emancipation, yet feeling the responsibility that fact bears with it, and the conditions on which alone Freedom can be a lasting blessing-- to give to these new-born citizens the right of a sound and healthful Christian education. The element of such training must be such as are fitted to any, white or black, who are in their mental and moral condition. They are not to be taught as if they are to abide an inferior race, free in name, but really slaves forever. Nor are they to have such training as to make them forget, in their freedom, that they are to obey the laws of God and man; to be thrifty, sober, chaste, and honest. In a word, such education in the solid branches of a good American school should be given them, as well fit them in due time for all civil and social callings they shall be found capable of. [7]

I believe we can safely assume that such education consisted primarily of instruction that the teachers felt was necessary for the blacks to be both better citizens and Christians. Yet the Commission also expanded upon this central goal of education and declared that it also intended to relieve the suffering of the freedmen and provide financial aid to those clergymen working with the freedmen. [8] These three areas--education, relief, and missionary salaries--would be the foci for all future Home Missions Commission work.

The Home Missions Commission enthusiastically began its task. The bishops of North Carolina, Tennessee, the South West, and other southern dioceses were asked to submit recommendations as to how the Commission should proceed with its work among the freedmen in general and in their dioceses in particular. The Commission did not want to offend any diocesan bishops. Notices were placed in newspapers seeking teachers to work among the freedmen; pamphlets were prepared explaining the work of the Commission; circulars were sent to the clergy, especially those residing in the dioceses of New York and Western New York; the missionary publication of the Episcopal Church, the Spirit of Missions, was used to send reports of the Commission's work to Episcopalians; and purchases of clothing at government sales were made, so the clothing could be shipped to the freedmen. The Rev. Brinton Smith was hired as the secretary and general agent; he worked

in the New York office. [9]

Off to a quick start, the Home Missions Commission
members were confident that they could make an impact, and it
seems that their enthusiasm was justified, because it was
reported at a later meeting in 1866 that the bishops welcomed
their efforts:

> The correspondence was almost without exception,
> of a satisfactory and gratifying character...and
> the result was that the dioceses of Virginia,
> North Carolina, Florida, Tennessee, Kentucky and
> the South West Missionary District, were opened to
> the labors of the Commission; not only so, but
> those labors have been welcomed, and in them we
> shall have the support and co-operation of the
> Bishop and very many of the Clergy. [10]

The Commission members believed that their prayers were being
answered and that with the support of the southern bishops,
the clergy and laity also would support this important cause.
All the Commission needed now was money to fund its projects.

The Home Missions Commission attempted to raise money
by asking that the clergy take up a collection on the
forthcoming Thanksgiving Day, that clothing be collected,
that special parish and diocesan auxiliaries be formed whose
expressed purpose was the aid of the freedmen, and that the
corresponding secretary "issue an appeal" informing the
Church of the commission's objectives. [11]

Members of the Commission probably hoped to build upon
the good will that the Rev. Francis Wharton, an executive
committee member, created when he actively spread the news of

the Commission's work, in the New York City area, during the last months of 1865. His message was straightforward: the freedmen must be helped. The appeal contained the standard reasoning of the day in that Mr. Wharton stressed the fearful consequences that unaided, uneducated freedmen would have on the society, and the moral responsibility of the white Christians to help this "debased race." The appeal was certainly racist, by today's standards, but it was no more or less racist than any other appeal made by either religious or secular authorities. But Mr. Wharton's appeal also had a nationalistic theme. He believed that in serving the blacks the whole country would be served. The Commission's mission was to rescue the blacks in order to save the country from a certain and terrifying destruction. He insisted:

> 'The Indians were a nomadic race, comparatively
> few in numbers, dwelling on our outskirts,
> instinctively wandering forth to die where their
> deaths wrought no paroxysm in the dominant
> society, and their corruption spread no infection.
> But the negro is not nomadic; he refused to wander
> from his old homes; there have these four millions
> of human beings lived, and there will they die.
> If they die from demoralization and degradation,
> ... this cannot but be degradation and debasement,
> if not death to ourselves. No nation can be
> prosperous, or healthy, or free, that palpitates
> with such death-throes as these, and incorporates
> such a polluting, dying presence.' [12]

The only antidote to such a deadly poison in the society was secular and religious education which could civilize and transform the blacks.

"Right-minded sons and daughters of the Church" were

hired as teachers whose duty it was to impart academic knowledge and to "disarm prejudice" and "conciliate the kindly feelings" of the freedmen. [13] The Commission never defined what it meant by "right-minded sons and daughter." I believe we can assume that it meant Church members of good character who believed God had called them to be teachers of the blacks. Teachers applied to the Commission for appointment and were expected to have a letter of reference. It is clear that the Commission was not about to accept just anyone. In any case, the Commission hired teachers and opened schools (1866) in Richmond, Norfolk, Halifax County, and Petersburg, Virginia; Newbern, Wilmington, and Raleigh, North Carolina; Sumter and Winnsboro, South Carolina; Louisville, Kentucky; and Okolona, Mississippi. Money was also given to the Colored Orphanage in Memphis, Tennessee. [14] By the end of 1866, the Commission had twenty-three teachers in the field and over 1600 students. [15]

The Commission never stated what prejudice they wanted the teachers to disarm. However after receiving freedom, the blacks immediately claimed their independence by worshipping in churches of their own choice. Ninety percent of the blacks in the Episcopal Church left to become members of their own black churches. [16] This upset the leadership of the Episcopal Church because they believed their denomination could serve the worship and faith needs of the black populace. The leaders were also fearful because the blacks

were joining what I might call "non-reasoning" churches. The missionaries, in describing the religion of the blacks, would refer to the emotionalism and unreasonableness of the services. One teacher reported to Spirit of Missions this exchange when she asked a student to be baptized in the Episcopal Church:

> Providence permitting, we are hoping to have a larger number of children baptized, also some for confirmation, next Sunday. I asked one of my brightest and best--a lad of seven years--if he would like to be baptized. He replied, "Yes, ma'am, I wants to be, but mother says if I'se baptized now, I'se'll grow up and not get converted, and then I'se'll die and the boogars (how do you spell it) will get me." There was a really sad expression upon the little fellow's face as he repeated it. I feel confident in saying that he will be brought into Christ's eternal fold. The task may be difficult, but by no means hopeless. It is the earnest desire of my heart to win the poor deluded ones to better and worthier living. [17]

Such worship experiences as "conversion" were foreign and incomprehensible to the Commission membership and to the missionaries. They believed the reasoned worship of the Episcopal Church was more beneficial to all of humanity than the emotional and frenzied worship of the black churches. Therefore a crusade was launched to rescue the Africans from the barbaric, emotional religion to which they were so attracted. The primary weapon was education. The Commission firmly believed: "Without education, and above all, without the knowledge of God in Christ, they must perish from the face of earth, or drag out a miserable existence, sinking

lower and lower in degradation and depravity." [18] Only the Episcopal Church could save the blacks from their degradation and depravity.

Throughout its twelve-year history, the Commission always stressed education, an education beneficial to the freed blacks and to the Church. Blacks were to be taught essential academic skills in order to provide them with skills to live in the larger, white society and because these same skills would encourage them to become members of the Church. Every educated freedman was a potential Episcopalian! Thus, education was a tool for evangelism and conversion. The missionaries knew that uneducated blacks could not understand or appreciate the Episcopal liturgy, so the missionary viewed education as the miracle which would remove the scales from the freedmen's eyes. New eyes and new visions would allow the blacks to see the greatness and glory of the Episcopal Church. An example of this can seen in a report from Mrs. Hall of the Mission School at Fayetteville, North Carolina who said of one student: "One of my favorite girls, who has been a regular attendant of the school for about two years and has been very exemplary in all things, about a month ago took charge of one of the district schools. She commenced with a primer. She is a young married woman, and became a Communicant last year. I mention her with pride." [19] Time and time again, a missionary would talk about her students and then go on to say how many had been

brought into the Church. Teachers clearly saw the classroom as a tool of evangelism.

Schools were established throughout the South. The Commission was able to provide the schools with funding for programs but was forbidden by the bylaws of the Domestic and Foreign Missionary Society to provide money for buildings. [20] The local school officials were responsible for raising their own money to build school buildings. In 1867 the Commission had 62 teachers and 4,016 students in an unspecified number of schools. The number grew to thirty-seven schools, 55 teachers, and a unreported number of students in 1877. [21] These schools were concerned with both the secular and religious education of the students. It was not until 1875 that the Commission turned its attention away from secular education and began to devote its energy to preparing men for a theological education. [22] It did so because the Church knew that it needed black missionaries to evangelize the black people, and because the state schools were providing an education that was "sufficient for the positions they are likely to occupy." [23] This change also illustrates that the Church leadership was no longer fearful that this newly, freed race would contaminate the society with its barbarous and superstitious behavior. Black missionaries had been desired for a long time, but the Commission did not make it a top priority until ten years after the emancipation.

Despite the high ratio of students to teachers, the shortage of supplies, the make-shift classrooms, and the sporadic student attendance, learning took place. In 1867 there was one teacher for every 64 students and many teachers allowed their advanced students to teach other students. [24] Teachers also complained of classrooms being too small or even of not having any classrooms at all and of having few or no supplies. One of the biggest complaints was the migrant nature of the families; they moved around so much that the teacher hardly had time to make an impression upon them. [25] Often the teachers were overworked; one taught black adults who lived in an isolated area on his day off and when asked to teach their children, promised to do so during his vacation. Hardly an ideal situation, but it shows the commitment that both the teachers and the students had to this ill-equipped and over-burdened system of schools. But teacher after teacher reported great progress, progress that was good no matter the age of the child or adult. Some of the students only had the time, talent, or inclination to learn what the teachers considered to be the rudimentary skills: the Lord's Prayer, Catechism, short sections from the Bible, perhaps some writing. Others went on to study in more depth. But no matter the amount of learning received, the teachers expressed great pride in their "scholars." This ignorant, supposedly unteachable race, was both intelligent and teachable. [26]

Of all the missions and schools that the Episcopal Church operated, it was the St. Augustine's Normal School in Raleigh, North Carolina that the Church seemed to appreciate the most. It was here that students eventually prepared not only to teach but also to become ordained ministers. St. Augustine's had its start in 1867 when an endowment of $25,000 was obtained from the estate of the late Charles Avery of Pittsburg, Pennsylvania. [27] He stated in his will that a large sum of his money was to be used for the education of blacks in the United States and Canada. General Howard of the U.S. Freedmen's Bureau was instrumental in convincing the trustees of the estate to award the money to St. Augustine's School. [28] This money enabled the school's trustees to buy land and to erect school buildings. By 1877 the school principal, the Rev. J. E. C. Smedes, reported that St. Augustine's owned ninety acres of land, had buildings worth $20,000 and had bonds, secured by mortgages and collateral, valued at $47,981. The school had thirty-eight boarding students, eighteen male and twenty female, as well as eighty-two day students. In addition to the principal, there were three salaried teachers and one matron. [29]

This institution saw itself as an elite school whose students were destined to teach and lead other blacks. Not only were the students required to study geography, grammar, arithmetic, natural sciences, spelling, reading, and writing, but the principal also reported that the students mastered

Goodwin's Greek Grammar and Reader, read six orations of
Cicero and Sallust's Jugurtha and Catiline, began Homer, and
mastered algebra and linear geometry. [30] The school
boasted in 1875 that it was the "only endowed church-school"
in the country that accepted black children and adults as
both day and boarding students and undertook to give them
advanced training. [31] Apparently others within the black
community realized this was an excellent institution for
learning; the principal reported in 1875 that seventy-six of
its past graduates were in teaching positions, and in 1876
Bishop Holly, Bishop of Haiti, visited the institution to
place his two sons and a young Haitian in the school. In
this same year, the institution had ten men preparing for the
ordained ministry, with four more planning to enter St.
Augustine's the next year. [32] The principal referred to the
school as a "handmaid" of the Episcopal Church because it
trained black men who were to "acceptably minister the Gospel
to our home-born Africans in the South." [33]

St. Augustine's School seems to have been the most
successful school for the blacks. It had a high standard of
education and apparently turned many students away because it
did not have a large enough endowment to cover the number of
students who needed full or half scholarships. Its success
was primarily due to its ability to secure financial reserves
which enabled it to meet the costs of running an educational
institution for a people who generally could not pay for

their own education. There were other schools which had
dedicated teachers and which strived for educational
excellence, but they did not have the economic support to
allow them to grow and prosper. It was money which
determined how successful the Church would be in ministering
to the freed blacks. Unfortunately, the Home Missions
Commission never had enough money to finance all of its many
programs.

In its first year, $26,106 dollars were given to the
Commission, of which it spent $24,723. The treasurer noted
that the Commission needed $100,000 for the next year and in
reality could spend two or three times that amount. [34]
However, the money did not appear. In 1868 the Commission
received only $28,663.86, and the treasurer had loaned the
Commission over $2500 so that its work could be accomplished.
Instead of spending $100,000 per year, only $90,000 was spent
between the Commission's formation and the end of 1868. [35]
The Commission's enthusiasm was not supported by Episcopal
congregations. The Commission reported that this average
sum of $30,000 dollars per year meant that the church members
were contributing less than one cent for each freedman. The
Commission was clearly disturbed that the local congregations
were not supporting this program with both their hearts and
money.

The Commission could not understand why Episcopalians
were reluctant to give them money. They did not realize that

the Commission's dream of helping the blacks was not shared by the average Episcopalian. As long as the black people did not bother the whites, the whites were content to forget about them and let them live in their own world. Certainly the whites had not seen the blacks as fully human when they were held in bondage, so it was difficult for them to perceive them as human when they lived in freedom. The Church membership was no more callous in their feelings than the average American, and the racism of Episcopalians was also shared by Christians of other denominations, as well as non-Christians. The Commission members were a minority attempting to serve another minority. The majority of Episcopalians never felt compelled to help them in their endeavors.

Despite appeal after appeal for funds, large amounts of money did not pour in. Cent by cent, the money dribbled in and the Commission was forced to rely on the generosity of the Domestic and Foreign Missionary Society to supply it with funds. The average Episcopalian was not about to condone the Commission's activities with their contributions. Each year there was a lack of resources. The Commission was forced to go into debt, a liability they struggled to pay off; they resolved never to be in arrears again. This fear of debt probably arose because the Commission knew that it could not depend on the Church membership or the governing board of the Domestic and Foreign Missionary Society to support it, if

the Commission became deeply indebted. The Church membership did not care enough about the work to want to rescue it and the Commission did not want to provoke criticism either by incurring indebtedness or by spendthrift programs. It sensed that its work was not respected by the Church hierarchy and membership.

The lowly status of the Home Missions Commission is clearly seen when we compare the funding that was given to the Home Missions Commission and the Indian Commission. H. Peers Brewer reported in his article on the Freedman's Commission that when the Indian Commission was established in 1871, its monetary contributions were greater than that for the Home Missions Commission, which had been in existence for six years. [36] This is rather startling at first glance, but it underscores the rampant prejudice against blacks that was woven into the fabric of the national life. Indians were also discriminated against, were mistreated, but in a different way than the blacks. The whites had a fearful respect for the Indians while they only had disdain for the blacks. The Indian was a part of the United States; he represented the wild, untamed America which God called the whites to conquer. Jordan Winthrop in White Over Black says:

> The Indian became for Americans a symbol of their
> American experience; it was no mere luck of the
> toss that placed the profile of an American Indian
> rather than an American Negro on the famous old
> five-cent piece. Confronting the Indian in
> America was a testing experience, common to all
> the colonies. Conquering the Indian symbolized
> and personified the conquest of the American

difficulties, the surmounting of the wilderness.
To push back the Indian was to prove the worth of
one's own mission, to make straight in the desert
a highway for civilization. With the Negro it was
utterly different. [37]

Whites saw the Indians as part of their country and therefore would contribute money for their education and evangelization. Work among the blacks was a mistake that Church members would not support with their time or money.

In 1874 only one dollar out of twenty-five contributed to the Domestic and Foreign Mission's Board of Missions was given for the work of the Home Missions Commission, and between 1865 and the demise of the Commission in 1878, Episcopalians gave only $325,278 to this ministry. [38] The lack of money had a profound, demoralizing effect on the Commission. In the annual report of 1873 the secretary wrote:

The apathy in regard to the object of our labors,
manifesting itself so decidedly in the great
neglect of our Missions, and in this refusal
(tacit at least) to send us aid, makes the duty of
your Commission any thing but light and pleasant;
on the contrary, it is wearying and painful; and
the Executive Committee has been at times tempted
to ask that they might be relieved of their burden
of duty and care. [39]

Despite such hardships, the Commission's membership remained faithful to their cause, and the Commission's objectives were met. Its membership truly believed that the Commission had a purpose and a mission among the freedmen of

the South. This was clearly illustrated in an article printed in the Spirit of Missions when Robert B. Minturn, the executive committee's treasurer, died in 1866. The article bemoaned not just the loss of a devoted Churchman, but the loss of a man who was committed to helping the freed blacks. He was the Commission member who stood for hours waiting to buy surplus government clothes to be sent to the freedman, and he was the one who urged the executive committee on with its work, so that the suffering of the freedmen might be somewhat alleviated. [40] The Home Missions Commission for Colored People was able to do as much as it did because of people like Robert Minturn, people who believed that they were doing God's will, in spite of human opposition and institutional obstacles.

Church members, private citizens, and newspapers both supported and opposed the work of the Home Missions Commission. There was enough debate about the Commission's objectives and work that the Commission rebutted the challenges and once again stated its goals, all the while regretting that it had been caught in the "cross fires" of differing opinions. [41] An editorial in Spirit of Missions stated that such differences of opinion were to be expected and that the Commission would have ignored the comments had they not come from "influential quarters." [42] The editorial continued:

An article from the Church Intelligencer, of Charlotte, N. C., opposes the National Bureau, but

upholds the Commission on the ground that it is
under the guidance of Southern bishops and clergy.
Another notice in the Church Review has its
peculiar style of interpretation as to the purpose
and methods of the Commission. On the other side,
the Episcopal Recorder, has in two numbers cited
remarks of Southern papers and uttered grave
doubts whether the Commission be true to the cause
of the colored man. [43]

Letters were also sent to the Commission questioning

whether the money sent to aid the blacks was "wholly"

administered by the southern Clergy; in a similar fashion

southern correspondents worried that the Commission might

bypass the southern clergy altogether. [44] The Commission

found itself caught in the conflict of opposing

understandings and conceptions of its task. The Church

leadership and membership could not agree on how to best

conduct its ministry to the blacks and therefore carefully

watched the activities of the Commission. It became a

sitting duck, an easy target for the different factions to

attack. This conflict reflected the divergent views of the

country itself. No one was sure as to the best way to

incorporate the blacks into the American mainstream. There

could be no agreement because many whites did not want the

blacks to be a part of their world.

Suspicion lingered about the Commission's work, giving

impetus to the people who wished to reform the manner in

which the Commission conducted its business. The Commission

was directly responsible for hiring and overseeing the work

of its teachers. Although the Commission only sent teachers to dioceses that requested and wanted their help, some critics questioned why the bishops were not fully in charge. Certainly, the diocesan bishops had directed all missionary activity in the past. Why was this ministry to the blacks any different from past endeavors or or even present missionary endeavors occurring among non-blacks? Critics argued that the Commission's independence eroded the traditional rights of the bishops. Consequently the Board of Missions, in 1870, changed its procedures and allowed the local bishop to select the missionaries for his diocese.[45] This action allowed the bishop to control the ministry to the blacks in his diocese. Probably the work benefited from this changed because it allowed people who understood the local conditions to choose people who might best work in those particular environments. However, this change also allowed the diocesan missionary endeavors to be tainted with local racial prejudices. No longer did the teachers and blacks have an authority far removed from their situation who could objectively examine the ministry conducted in the local setting. I believe this change weakened the effectiveness of the Commission and occurred because southern Church leaders were afraid that the Commission might encourage the blacks to yearn for too much freedom. After all, who would better know the delicate balance of the social environment than the southern bishops? The last thing the white southern bishops

wanted was the black populace further upsetting their world.

Another blow to the integrity of the Commission came in
1877 when Bishop Bedell of Ohio charged the Board of Missions
with violating the Church's canons by creating within the
Board of Missions four branches of work: foreign, domestic,
colored, and Indian. He insisted that the Church had decreed
that there should be only two fields of missionary endeavor:
foreign and domestic. Protesting that the current structure
wasted money, he asked: "Are the difficulties of Indian
Mission, and Mission to Colored People of the South, too
great to be mastered by noble men whom the Spirit of God has
sent to guide the Dioceses where these problems exist?" [46]
Such questioning undoubtedly arose, because of financial
concerns, since some church members questioned the amount of
money that the Board of Missions spent on administration.
However there may be another reason as well: racism.
Certainly Bishop Bedell was concerned about the effectiveness
of the Church's missionary programs, but, as the
aforementioned quote illustrates, he could not discern why
the blacks or Indians needed any special help from the
Church. He boldly stated that what was good enough for the
whites was good enough for the blacks and Indians. Such
statements reflected the attitude of many of the nations's
citizens. They also reflect a subtle racism which refused to
acknowledge racial differences, because to acknowledge such
differences meant that whites had to examine how they treated

people of different races. Pretending that there were no differences allowed people to remain blind to their own prejudices.

Mr. William Welsh, a member of the Executive Committee of the Indian Commission, answered Bishop Bedell's criticism by saying he was willing to discuss structural changes but warned that radically changing the current organization could lead to disastrous results for the missionary endeavors among the Indians and Freedmen. He urged Bishop Bedell and others to remember that "as long as these prejudices exist, and as long as many liberal contributors to the Foreign Committee and to Missions, white men would, through prejudice, withhold their contributions, if a portion of them were likely to be appropriated to the red man or black man...." [47] His protests were to no avail. The Home Missions Commission to the Colored People was dissolved and its affairs were placed under the leadership and direction of the Domestic and Foreign Missionary's domestic missions department by order of the General Convention in 1877. The new mission bylaws clearly stated that the missionary field "is always to be regarded as one--THE WORLD," and declared that there were to be only two organizational branches for missionary work: domestic and foreign. [48]

Work among the blacks continued but without much direction or encouragement. Local dioceses decided what ministry occurred, so the Church's ministry varied from

diocese to diocese. This casual and diffuse ministry was questioned by some Church leaders who wanted the Episcopal Church to be more systematic and involved in its ministry to the blacks. Consequently, the General Convention of 1886 created a whole new body called the Commission for Work among Colored People. We will look at this Commission in more detail in a following chapter. However, the reason for its creation is important. The Episcopal Church believed that it had neglected the needs of the black; it declared the Commission was formed "...to awaken the Church to the importance of work among colored people in the South...." [49]

People outside of the Church questioned not just the structure of the Home Missions Commission but also whether the Episcopal Church should be working among blacks in the first place. We saw inferences of this when we talked about the criticism leveled against the Commission in the various newspapers. Criticism also arose from the black community. Some blacks, especially black pastors, felt that they did not need the help of Episcopal Church. The Rev. Giles B. Cooke of St. Stephen's Parish in Petersburg, Virginia was very critical of those he called "so-called spiritual pastors" who stirred up ill-feelings toward the ministry of the Episcopal Church. He accused these pastors of stirring up racial prejudice and said they "...plainly teach their congregations that there is no religion in the Episcopal Church. They

carry their opposition to our Church so far that they threaten to turn away any member of their Churches for permitting their children to attend our Sunday-School." [50] The Rev. W. K. Douglas of Dry Grove, Mississippi also reported that the blacks were suspicious of his ministry and stated that the Baptist preachers tried to turn the Episcopal Sunday school into a Baptist one. But at a community meeting to elect trustees for the public school, the blacks unanimously decided to keep the Sunday school under the direction of the Episcopal Church. He remarked that he was greatly surprised because he had supposed that he had lost the Sunday school to the Baptists. [51] This incident demonstrates that the blacks were capable of deciding their own future and did not want to be dictated to by any group. Help was important, but not nearly as important as their personal and corporate freedom.

The school teachers and missionaries sent by the Home Missions Commission were not interested in the personal and corporate freedom of the blacks. They were interested in getting them to adhere to white, middle class values. Salvation for the blacks meant their acceptance of these values. Consequently, the teachers were insensitive to the cultural gifts that the blacks could bring to the Episcopal Church and the larger white world. The teachers typically saw the black values as alien and foreign, attitudes that had to be erased in order for true Christian virtues to grow and

mature. No matter the cost to teacher or pupil, the teachers

were determined that the blacks should change and become

Episcopalized. We find such attitudes in a letter sent to

the Spirit of Missions by Miss Aiken, a teacher at

Petersburg, Virginia. She described her experiences at a

black revival meeting. A white preacher first addressed the

crowd; she did not like his remarks. Then the crowd began to

sway and sing hymns. She reported:

> The scene then became intensely fascinating, and
> one felt inclined to join the swaying element. We
> stood upon our seats to overtop the crowd.
> Nothing disturbed them, but all seemed bound by
> the spirit of the hour. Suddenly one of the
> 'mourners' sprang up, shouting, leaping and
> shaking hands, as if an evil spirit, rather than a
> good one, possessed him, proclaiming joy and
> gladness for the pardon of his sins in the most
> frantic manner. Some endeavored to calm him;
> others cried 'Let him talk! 'twill do him good! I
> know how he feels.' As I looked upon the vast sea
> of ignorance before me my heart melted with pity,
> and I was deeply impressed with the conviction
> that even 'the least' in our Church can do much in
> this great work which lies before her. [52]

The feelings expressed in this letter were typical of

most Home Missions Commission teachers and were typical of

the average white American; the whites did not like,

appreciate, or understand the black culture. They saw it

devoid of all civilized beauty and goodness. The blacks were

different from the whites; the skin color was just an outer

reflection of a deeper difference. The whites questioned

whether the blacks could ever be transformed into educated,

honest, and productive citizens. However, in spite of the

misunderstandings, in spite of the blacks and whites living in two different worlds, in spite of the racial prejudices, the whites and blacks needed one another. The blacks needed economic and educational assistance and the whites needed to give them this help. The help given to the blacks may not have always been the very best and may have been insensitive and even cruel, but such attempts at helping the blacks opened the door for future contacts between the races. ·It set a precedence that said to one and all: Whites and Blacks can work together, live together, worship together,and even learn together.

But before we end our discussion about the Church's first ministry to the freed blacks, I believe we should take a brief look at the role of women with the Home Missions Commission. Women did not hold official, organizational power; there were no female officers of this commission. However, its major accomplishments were created by the dedication and labor of women. Most teachers were women, and it was these teachers who were the educational missionaries of the Episcopal Church. They were the ones who dealt with the tremendous needs of their black constituents and attempted to sensitize the Church to the pressing demands of this oppressed population. But their endeavors and sacrifices were taken for granted. Teachers were needed, women were teachers, and therefore it was assumed that women would venture forth into these domestic missionary fields. It

was the contact of the white "minority" with the black "minority" which proved to be beneficial to the Church's missionary endeavors. The Home Missions Commission could not have existed without the help, work, and support of women.

One exception to the inclusion of female leadership within the Home Missions Commission arose when the Pennsylvania Branch of the Home Missions Commission was organized at St. Luke's Church, Philadelphia, on 24 November 1866. [53] This auxiliary to the Home Missions Commission was formed to help the freedmen by improving their education and providing them with other necessary needs, such as clothing. This was an organization that was expressly for women, and the original announcement of its organization was directed to the women of parishes in the dioceses of Eastern & Western Pennsylvania, Delaware, and South New Jersey. [54] Later this organization would state that it was open to all sexes, but the vast majority of its membership remained female. Its first and only president was Isabelle James (Mrs. Thomas P. James); however, there were also male "counselors" connected with this group. [55] These counselors were primarily the rectors of local congregations who supported the women and their work and who asked their colleagues to read an explanatory letter about the group's purposes to their congregations. [56]

The society was created because the members believed the Episcopal Church was without equal in being able to help

the freedmen. While they encouraged help from every quarter, it was the Episcopal Church that could and would provide the right help for the newly freed slaves. In their flyer inviting women to join the Pennsylvania Branch, they asserted: "...Our Church has peculiar advantages and facilities for education, and can supply the highest form of instruction in developing the entire man, spirit, mind, and body.... We have no antagonism towards other instrumentalities but desire to employ that which...seems to us the best and most efficient." [57] Women were asked to form auxiliaries of the branch within their congregations and to send a representative to Philadelphia each month for the Board of Managers meeting. [58]

The formation of the Pennsylvania Branch encouraged the Home Missions Commission to dream that other branches could arise throughout the country. An editorial in the January 1867 edition of Spirit of Missions said:

> Ladies have more influence than gentlemen in works
> of benevolence and money, and they can do more
> than any agency to awaken and sustain an interest
> in the particular field in which we are engaged.
> If we could get a sufficient number of ladies to
> inaugurate and carry forward branches of our
> Commission in New York, Boston, Providence,
> Buffalo, Pittsburg, Cincinnati, and Chicago, we
> doubt not our efficiency would be increase ten
> fold. [59]

The editor was quite correct. If the imagination of the Church's women could be turned toward this concern, the Church's work among the blacks would dramatically increase.

Evidence of this can be seen in the quick, initial successes of the Pennsylvania Branch. On 21 January 1867, Isabelle James reported that the organization of the branch had been impeded by the "Fairs and Festivals of the holiday season." [60] Yet in spite of the holiday the branch had mailed 2100 brochures describing the Church's work among the freedmen, mailed fifty letters to clergy requesting that Mrs. James be invited to speak to their female members, obtained seven speaking engagements for Mrs. James, formed auxiliary societies, received three applications from people desiring to be teachers, and garnered over a thousand dollars in money and contributions. All this took place in just two months after the branch's formation! [61] This momentum continued because Mrs. James reported in May of that same year that twenty-six auxiliaries had been formed, not including "contributing societies," and the Pennsylvania Branch was supporting thirteen teachers. [62] By the end of the year, the branch was supporting twenty four teachers, of which 13 were black. This branch alone supported 38% of the teachers that the Home Missions Commission employed in January 1868. [63]

These successes were short-lived. Economic troubles afflicted the country, and the Pennsylvania Branch found itself with a debt of $1600, of which $1200 was borrowed personally by Mrs. James. The debt arose because congregations were not able to pay all or some of the money

they had pledged. Money was borrowed so they could "pay the salaries of the teachers at their field of labor, and transfer them to their homes." [64] This organizational crisis deeply affected their enthusiasm, and the group resolved to be more conservative in their future dealings. Teachers were hired only when their "salaries were guaranteed by Church's making regular payments." [65] This limited their teachers to about five, and also affected the way in which the Pennsylvania Branch saw itself and its work. Instead of remaining a powerful force within the Home Missions Commission, it became a conduit for "guaranteed" money. There was no need for them to function in this manner because the official conduit for money was the Home Missions Commission. The Pennsylvania Branch folded in 1870 and referred all support and contributions to the Commission. [66]

The Home Missions Commission was successful in its endeavors, although perhaps not as much as it wanted to be. Teachers were hired, schools begun, congregations formed, and relationships established. The teachers and missionaries of this movement were heroes in their own right. They felt called by God to work among the blacks and help them gain respect and freedom in their new world. It was not any easy task and there were many broken promises and many failures. However, the teachers and missionaries did their best to be honest to themselves, their calling, and the black race. No

more can be asked of any people. This Commission laid the groundwork for future Church endeavors among the blacks and gave the Domestic and Foreign Missions Society the organization and missionaries to continue this vital ministry. [67]

But the Home Missions Commission could not remove the one obstacle that blocked its road to success--racial prejudice. Miss S.G. Swetland, Principal of St. Augustine's School in Newberne, North Carolina despairingly wrote:

> Would that the Church could realize the magnitude
> and importance of this work! Prejudice against
> any race must melt away under the warmth of Gospel
> influence; the common brotherhood will eventually
> be recognized. The mission of the Church is to
> instruct and elevate, irrespective of race or
> caste; nor is it for us to question as to 'common
> or unclean.' 'Who maketh thee to differ from
> another?' and what hast thou didst not receive?'
> Still, I am somewhat hopeless whilst I write. Our
> people generally will not take an adequate
> interest in this department of Mission work. I
> have ceased to expect it. Thousands of human
> beings at our doors--waiting, famishing
> souls--whilst our brethern are contesting as to
> political aspects; and refinement is shuddering
> with the fear of enforced equality. [68]

Her words were prophetic, for the Church membership never saw the black race as brothers and sisters in Christ.

Diocesan Ministry to the Freedmen, 1865 -1878

While the National Church, through the Home Missions
Commission, was striving to serve the needs of the blacks and
was both applauding its successes and lamenting its failures,
the Episcopal dioceses typically admitted that the blacks
should be helped, and then promptly ignored the blacks'
plight. I plan to look at the work and rhetoric of five
different dioceses throughout the South, ranging from the
boarderline-state of Maryland, to Virginia, North Carolina,
Tennessee, and Georgia. I chose these dioceses somewhat at
random and because the Home Missions Commission reported work
taking place in each of these dioceses, except for Maryland.

Very little was done to assist the black population of
Maryland from 1865 to 1878. Bishop Whittingham, the Bishop
of Maryland, devoted minimum attention to the freedmen in his
diocesan convention addresses. His diocesan address of 1866
urged the convention to review the Diocese's work among the
blacks. [1] The convention reacted, typically, by forming a
committee called the Committee on Freedmen. This committee
reminded the convention in 1867 that the blacks were part of
the Church, the church in which "there is neither Jew nor
Greek--there is neither slave nor free--there is neither male
nor female...." [2] Therefore the Church had a responsibility to minister to the blacks, and that if the Church

did not minister to the blacks "with the pure leaven of Christ's most Holy Gospel, they will either be brought under influences utterly godless, or such as our Branch of the Church of Christ cannot sanction." [3] The committee suggested that the best way of ministering to the freedmen was through raising up black pastors and teachers under the direction of the Episcopal Church "until they can be prepared to regulate their own Ecclesiastical affairs in communion with our Branch of the Church Catholic." [4] Such appeals did not convince the church membership that a ministry to the blacks was necessary. Little or nothing is mentioned about such ministry from 1867 to 1878. Clearly this project did not capture the imagination of the Diocese of Maryland.

In contrast to the apathy of the Diocese of Maryland, the Diocese of Virginia, at first, seemed to be very interested in helping the blacks. The Committee on Colored Congregations reported to the diocesan council in 1867 that its work had "progressed slowly indeed," but "they had experienced a "reasonable degree of success." [5] It reported specific ministries occurring in five or six locations across the diocese: Richmond, Norfolk, Petersburg, Halifax county, Hanover county, and Sussex County. [6] Establishment of Sunday schools, day schools, and black congregations was the main thrust of diocesan mission efforts. This strategy was successful, and the committee urged the Virginia Council to "increased attention to this

vastly important work." [7] The shining star was the mission project at Petersburg. In an eighteen month period, the Petersburg Sunday School numbered 300 students, the parish school had 465 registered students with 230 students attending classes on any given day. A building was purchased for the Sunday and Wednesday services, which were well attended. This ministry, however, was interrupted when the building was destroyed by fire. [8] Consequently both the congregation and the students "scattered," and the missionary work hampered. [9]

Mr. A. W. Wendell who was responsible for much of the mission work at Petersburg reported to the Virginian Council in 1868 that the work at Petersburg was prospering. The fire gave the diocese and local congregation the resolve to build an "independent" church, that is a structure for a separate, black Episcopal congregation. So with funds from the Freedmen's Bureau, the Home Missions Commission, the Pennsylvania Branch, and from many private individuals, a church was erected at a cost of $5,214. [10] This church was named St. Stephen's Episcopal Church. Mr. Wendell remarked that the new church was built because of the "the crowded attendance of the colored people at our Episcopal churches every Sabbath, and the manifest interest they exhibited in the Episcopal service. This fact has been noticed nowhere to such an extent as in Petersburg." [11] St. Stephen's came into union with the Diocese in 1869, although it did not have

the same rights as did the white congregations. [12] The congregation did not have a seat and voice, traditional rights given to every white congregation. Instead, a special Standing Council was elected and represented the congregation at the Council meetings and in other diocesan affairs. Even in the midst of a successful ministry among the blacks, the Diocese of Virginia was clear that it could not accept blacks as equals. The blacks could form Episcopal congregations, but such congregations were not granted the rights and privileges given to white congregations. The blacks were accepted as second-class Christians.

Virginia's interest in the blacks seemed to wane as it took the blacks and their problems for granted. Special missionary projects for blacks were seldom discussed at Virginia's Council meetings. However one matter of great importance concerned the Council: what relationship would black congregations with black pastors have with the entirely white Council? A committee was appointed in 1869 to to inquire how other southern dioceses handled this situation and to determine whether the Council needed to make special arrangements. The Rev. Dr. Andrews reported in 1871: "...it appeared that there were at the time but two congregations served by colored ministers, one in Virginia and one in Maryland, and that with respect to both, no special legislation had been called for by them, or dissatisfaction with existing with existing relationships expressed." [13]

The Council did not have to address this issue because black congregations with black pastors were the exception not the rule. The absence of black pastors is rather startling, if one remembers that the Freedmen's Committee of the Diocese of Maryland urged their convention in 1866 to begin planning for black pastors. However, we see within the Virginia's Council's concern a deep fear and dread. They did not want black congregations directly represented at their Council meetings. They were so fearful of such an event occurring that the Council wanted to prepare for it in advance! Their worries were unfounded. The nightmare of blacks and whites sitting together in the same room would not turn into reality because the Diocese was reluctant to have an aggressive ministry among the blacks; little work was reported between 1871 and 1878.

Conversely the Diocese of Georgia reported very little work among the blacks until the the 1870's. Bishop Beckworth in his annual report of 1873 reminded the diocese that the population of Georgia was over one million people with 400,000 of that number of the black race. [14] He suggested that the national Church should provide the dioceses with missionary bishops for the black people. He eloquently said: "If St. Paul was sent to the Gentiles and St. Peter to the Jews; if we send Bishops to the Whites in America and a Bishop to the Indians, why should we not send a Bishop to the colored people?" [15] But the national Church was not ready

to authorize special bishops to minister in jurisdictions that were already administered by existing white bishops.

The truth of the matter is that the Diocese of Georgia did not need special bishops; it needed more interested men and woman who were willing to work with the black population to build churches and schools. J. W. Leigh who ministered to the blacks in Darien, Georgia reported to Bishop Beckworth in 1876:

> The colored people of Darien are in earnest about the work, and are amongst the most respectable of their race in Darien. They only need a little encouragement and an energetic person to go amongst them, and to bring them into the true fold of the church. Such a person might be of their own color or white--a clergyman or a lay reader--any one in fact who is earnest in the work, and can bring them into the church. Above all, if only a good school could be started by the Episcopal Church, success would be ensured. [16]

This belief that the Episcopal Church could help the freedmen through the founding of schools was common place and would be the main focal point of both national and diocesan ministry.

The Diocese of Tennessee initiated its ministry by assuming control of a private orphanage for black children, the Colored Orphans' Asylum more commonly known as the Canfield Orphans' Asylum. This orphanage was begun by Mrs. Martha Canfield, an Episcopalian, and was located in the suburbs of Memphis, Tennessee. [17] It was, at first, independent of the Diocese, although Bishop Todd Quintard and others performed services at the orphanage and baptized the

children. Mrs. Canfield asked the Tennessee Convention in 1866 to assume total control of the orphanage. [18] The convention assumed responsibility of the orphanage but did not thoroughly consider how they would fund such a project because they were not prepared for the traditional sponsors of the orphanage to withdraw their monetary support creating "financial uncertainties." [19] There is no mention of who originally supported this orphanage or why the "incidental sources of supplies were withdrawn." [20] Three sources of action were quickly proposed by the Committee on Freedmen to the 1867 Convention: 1. A semiannual offering throughout the diocese in support of this institution 2. The adoption of these children by Episcopalians 3. The establishment of a permanent committee to oversee the orphanage. [21] These proposals were approved by the convention.

Bishop Quintard in his 1867 address to the convention praised Mrs. Canfield for her work with the black children. Inadvertently, he also predicted how the Diocese of Tennessee and the community would deal with this asylum: public acceptance and private rejection. He said in part:

> She has met with many obstacles, has borne many crosses, has found little sympathy, and yet has given time, energy, money, all that she could, to the work which God, in His wonderful providence, assigned her. Had she left family and friends to carry the consolations of the Gospel to the heathen in Africa, every generous heart would have applauded the noble sacrifice; and surely in a work of our own Church...our people should not stand aloof, but accord their countenance and support. [22]

The bishop would be disappointed by his diocese's reaction to this new project. The orphanage became a new cross for the bishop and diocese to bear.

Within three short years of the diocese assuming control of the Canfield Orphanage (1869), the director lamented the sad state of affairs and bitterly complained that to be associated with the orphanage was a "thankless position" since the community found the orphanage to be odious. [23] Financial problems were mounting; the matron was owed money but the director reported that she did not complain because of her great concern that the orphans be clothed and fed. The committee overseeing the orphanage also reported in 1869 that the institution had been supported by northern charities and the U.S. Government over the last four years and that only in the past year had any congregation or person within the diocese of Tennessee contributed money to the orphanage; this was true in spite of the resolution adopted by the convention in 1867 asking every parish to support this institution. [24] This "asylum" for homeless black children was very much, in the mind and demeanor of the diocese, an orphan that the diocese did not want to support.

Financial problems were not the only concerns facing this endeavor. Only twenty children were wards of the orphanage in 1869 and the committee began suggesting that the diocese should consider turning the orphanage into a school for adults and children. [25] The number of orphans dropped

to eighteen by the following year, but a free school for children had been established which had eighty students and as well as a Sunday school with one hundred students. Efforts to maintain the orphanage were eventually abandoned, and the buildings and grounds were used for a school for black children. [26]

In 1874, according to diocesan sources, one fourth of Tennessee's population was composed of black citizens, about 333,000 people. The reason put forth to aid this segment of the population was paternalistic and reflected common stereotypes of the day: "...Their claim upon us to contribute as far as we can towards their spiritual welfare, is confirmed and enforced by their previous history in the land, their cheerful services, by their fidelity, by their general harmlessness and patience in terms of adversity to the country and by their capacity for civic usefulness and religious advancement." [27] Ministry took place because the diocese believed the black race was helpless and unfortunate.

Tennessee, like others dioceses, came to the conclusion that only black pastors could reach the black people. A Committee on Work among Colored People reported that "itinerant colored ministers" were necessary for a successful ministry, and urged the convention to discuss and implement ways to educate "colored" candidates for holy orders and to develop financial support for such "colored" ministers. [28] I could not determine whether these proposals were passed by

the convention, but in 1875 there was no mention of "colored"
ministers or plans for their education and ordination. There
were references to three black parishes: 1. "A Parish" in
Memphis with twenty-five communicants; 2. St. Paul's in Mason
which had 150 communicants and was ministered to by a
"colored Deacon"; 3. St. Philip's, Bolivia, with fifteen
communicants under the direction of the Rev. Wm. C. Gray, a
white minister. [29] It was clearly one thing to talk about
the formation of black ministry and another to implement it.

The Diocese of North Carolina faced this same dichotomy
between action and rhetoric. Bishop Thomas Atkinson in 1866
told the convention that it was extremely important to obtain
"colored ministers" because other denominations would attempt
to evangelize the freedmen. He said in part:

> Shall we, like the Priest and Levite, see the
> wounded man lying half dead, and pass by on the
> other side, and leave him to be ministered to by
> some hated Samaritan? This would be to confute
> our own pretensions, and it is to be remembered
> with regard to this subject, as with regard to
> schools, that the question is not whether there
> shall be colored Ministers, but what sort of
> colored Ministers these shall be? [30]

We can wonder who the Samaritan was in Bishop Atkinson's
mind. It was most definitely any "hostile" or "foreign"
elements that might inflate the ego or fan the enthusiasms of
the black people. [31] The Bishop wanted the black people
influenced by the white, Episcopal mindset.

Even with the belief that the Church had an emergency

to deal with, very little was done to shape the black world or mind. A committee on the Education and Religious Instruction of the Colored People in 1867 declared that it was the Church's duty to help educate the freedman because education without moral and religious tenets was defective. This committee also stated: 1. There was an emergency; the educational needs of the blacks had to be dealt with immediately. 2. It was as much their duty to aid the blacks as it was for any other portion of the community. 3. The committee wanted to "correct, as far as possible, the improper, defective and erroneous education which will otherwise be imparted." [32] The convention, following the committee's suggestions, resolved that regular schools and Sunday schools were to be established in every parish, that colored ministers be employed, and that the Diocese be willing to accept funding from any and all sources to erect structures to help them perform this ministry. Once again, more was said then was accomplished.

One year later the only tangible result of this action was the formation of a normal school for the education of teachers and a training school for those preparing for holy orders. This Normal/Training School was established in Raleigh, North Carolina and was administered by J. Brinton Smith, the former secretary of the Home Missions Commission. [33] Additionally, schools and Sunday schools were opened in various parishes, but they never captured the interest of the

convention. Not much attention was given to black work. The parochial statistics conform this: In 1868 there were 1667 white catechumens and 1085 black catechumens and 2839 white communicants compared to 194 black communicants; in 1873 there were 3499 white communicants compared to 243 black, 2687 white Sunday school pupils and 523 black, 588 white parochial school children and 161 black children; in 1877 there were 4186 white communicants and 369 black communicants, 2544 white Sunday school pupils and 345 black; 120 white parochial school children and 330 black. [34] The Diocese of North Carolina was not successful in gaining black members or in influencing the general, black population.

Racial prejudice also distorted the ministry that was being offered to the blacks. One reason that Bishop Atkinson tinkered with the idea of embracing ritualistic movement, which was becoming popular in some English and U.S. congregations, was that he believed it would appeal to the "...large colored population, who are peculiarly liable to be affected by whatever appeals to the eye and ear." [35] However he dismissed ritualism as an effective means of evangelism because he was afraid that the black population would not be able to see beyond the ritual to the true doctrines of the Church; in other words, the blacks did not have the mental capabilities to deal with ritual that might distort Church teachings. A similar thought was expressed by the Assistant Bishop of North Carolina, Bishop Lyman, in 1875

when he stressed that the Church had an important mission to perform among the blacks because the Episcopal Church's worship contained "plain and simple" language, repetitive elements, and a "sober and chastening spirit." [36] It was clear that the majority of Episcopalians felt the blacks were child-like beings who need the help and support of the superior, Episcopal Church liturgy. It was not explained how such a "superior" liturgy could benefit both the intellectually strong and the intellectually weak.

With the belief that the Episcopal Dioceses could bring salvation to the black population arose a creeping bitterness: the Southern dioceses did not want to deal with the black population all by themselves. It was as much a northern problem as a southern one. After all, every white had benefited from the blacks' long years in slavery. Now, the whole country, and especially the whole Church should help solve the problems of "Episcopalizing" the black population. Bishop Lyman insisted that the church in North Carolina could never fulfill its obligations to the blacks "unless we can have the sympathy and liberal cooperation of our brethren at the North." [37] The Church in North Carolina had, by 1875, ceased to be seriously concerned about ministering to the black population. It was no different than any other Episcopal Diocese; all had ceased to actively and aggressively minister to the black race. It is little wonder then that the General Convention in 1886 felt that a

new, national Church commission had to be created.

CHURCH COMMISSION FOR WORK AMONG COLORED PEOPLE, 1887-1904

The life of the Home Missions Commission to Colored People ended with the passage of a new Missionary Canon in 1877. [1] The reason for its demise was stated to be a reorganization of the Domestic Missions Department in order to save money and to emphasize that there were no divisions among the Church's missionary endeavors; from this point in 1877 there would only be two missionary departments: foreign and domestic. Some critics of the missionary department found even this division artificial; there could only be one field of endeavor, the world! Yet, the General Convention still thought it was wise at least to organize its work between the two departments so that the mission work could be well managed and efficiently run.

This reorganization of the missions department meant that the commissions which formerly administered the affairs of the black people and the American Indians were swallowed up, assumed by the Domestic Missions department; they became subdivisions within that department. Such a move was certainly in concord with Church sentiment that the Missions department had to be streamlined and that no particular mission department should be emphasized. But, the assumption of the commissions' responsibilities did not create an increase in the number of people working in the Domestic

Missions department. Additional employees were not hired because the Domestic Missions department was sensitive to the general feeling among Church leaders that administrative costs had to be kept low. Such financial concerns partly explain why the Commission for Home Missions was eliminated in the first place. The General Convention was convinced that the Home Missions' work could be done by the Domestic Missions department for less money without a loss of productivity or efficiency. Also, some Church members feared the growth of competition among the three executive departments: Domestic (White), Colored, and Indian. Such competition was counter to their understanding of the Church. The Episcopal Church was a unified Church, with unified members. Any competition for funds or power was not in keeping with their understanding of what the Church was and what it would be in the future. Competition was divisive and had to be eliminated. The Rev. A. T. Twing, Secretary of the Domestic Missions, approved of the reorganization and proudly stated:

> This consolidation of executive departments has brought no small additional amount of work to the Domestic office, but not such an increase as to demand an increased number of employes. The three branches of actual Mission work, each with its own peculiarities and each bright with promise, are distinct as before....
> The consolidation of the three executive departments of the Domestic work is in the line of economy in expenditure upon appliances, and in the line of unity also; and so far it is well, and merits general approval. With three executive departments, working in the same general field, there was a danger of misunderstanding and

unfriendly complications. There is negative gain
in the removal of this possible source of evil.[2]

We must question whether the evil of divisiveness was

not itself raised because of a much deeper and more

persuasive evil, that of racial discrimination. The Rev.

Wellington Webb, the secretary of the Home Missions

Commissions, wrote in an editorial in the Spirit of Missions

in 1878 that the work of the Home Missions Commission had

been questioned "every autumn, for several years past..." and

that the missions department was almost evenly divided over

the issue. [3] His editorial tone was one of relief; that

finally the issue had been settled and the work could

continue. But he never publicly confronted the reason for

the dissension. I believe the work was questioned because

the general membership of the Church was always as

uncomfortable with the program as they were with the black

race in general. They did not know how to treat these former

slaves. They could grudgingly admit they were human beings,

but they could never quite admit that they were equal. The

black people could not be their equals; they were inferiors

whom God had ordained to be enslaved and had been given to

the United States population as a burden, a responsibility

they had to endure. An Episcopal bishop wrote in 1894:

> I think the greatest difficulty we have to contend
> with lies in the fact, that the two races are in a
> transition stage regarding their relations to each
> other. The older people whites and blacks, are
> most intimately and oft times most lovingly

associated with each other. Not so the younger
people. No sooner was the Negro proclaimed free,
than he began to ask himself the question: How
can I keep and enlarge my freedom? The young
whites as naturally asked: How can we keep this
untutored mass from corrupting our most sacred and
cherished inheritances, social, moral, and
political. [4]

Church members could verbally say they wanted to help these

newly freed citizens, but deep within they would not and

could not help them. Episcopalians were afraid that their

world order would crumble; they were afraid the blacks would

contaminate the Anglo-Saxon race.

This deep-seated fear is seen in an 1878 Spirit of

Missions editorial that centered around the election of a

state senator in the 18th senatorial district of the state of

Georgia. The editorial describes a gathering of blacks

listening to the prospective candidates state their various

platforms. The editor was horrified that these black people

would cast the decisive votes to determine who would be the

next state senator. His horror was based on his belief that

"...those who, through no fault of theirs, are least

qualified for the responsible trust...." [5] The question

is, when would the white Episcopalians ever believe that the

blacks were qualified? No references were made in regard to

uneducated whites casting unqualified votes. Qualification

had more to do with the color of the skin than it did with

intellectual capabilities.

The Church was blind to its own prejudice. Its programs reflected this blindness because they both attempted to lift up the blacks and yet keep them inferior. The Church determined that the blacks were to see the world with the eyes of the Anglo-Saxon, for his eyes were the most perfect of all. Of course the blacks could never be Anglo-Saxons and thus could never measure up to such expectations. No matter how much help was given to the blacks, they never seemed to rise above their immoral and barbaric ways. Bishop Lyman said in 1883:

> As to moral and religious progress, I think there has been scarcely any, and in most districts there has been a positive deterioration. And we need not wonder at this, for nearly all the so-called religious teachers are colored men who have very small amount of education, and very little knowledge of the doctrines and principles of Christianity, and who are therefore entirely incompetent to be the guides and teachers of others. Now the natural result of all this is the general prevalence of ideas in relation to the Gospel system which are utterly and fatally false. [6]

Bishop Lyman's interpretation of the black people's plight was typical of the way Church members perceived the black situation. They attempted to help because they were members of a Catholic church, and if they did not help, they could not claim the title of "Catholic." [7] After all, Christ died to save all peoples and therefore the Church had a responsibility to serve all peoples. Such a theology did propel the Church into a ministry to the blacks; however, it

was a ministry that was without direction and varied from
diocese to diocese. This was especially true when the
General Convention decided that the Home Missions Commission
should no longer be a separate division of the Missions
department. Its merger into the Domestic Missions office
meant that the Church's ministry to the blacks lost its
direction because there were no vocal advocates for this
missionary work. Work did occur, but it occurred at the will
and the whim of the various dioceses. Such work was not
effective because it was not really responsible to any one
organization and there was no substantial support system for
the missionaries. [8] The missionaries were frustrated by
the lack of guidance and by the Church's general lack of
interest in their work.

They refused to give up. It was the missionaries out
in the field who reminded the Church over and over again that
there was a real thirst for the Gospel in the United States.
Reports to the Spirit of Missions conveyed a message of
neglect, despair, and bewilderment. The missionaries could
not understand why the Church was so silent and aloof about
this important ministry. They offered practical suggestions
as to how to improve and further their ministry, but their
comments were almost universally ignored. They asked for
money for buildings, for school supplies, for the
establishment of free churches in which both poor whites and
blacks could worship together. [9] One poignantly reminded

the Church that the black people would not disappear, even if
the Anglo-Saxons hoped they would: "The black people are
citizens. They are Americans. They are among us. They are
here permanently, and our duty is plain. We neglect it at
our peril." [10]

Missionaries also reported that the blacks wanted their
own separate churches.   The missionary correspondence
sometimes indicated that the blacks wanted separate places of
worship more so than the white missionaries. The Rev. D. B.
Waddell of Union Springs, Alabama reported:

> ...It is impracticable and unreasonable to try to
> force the two races to worship together. The
> colored race, even more than the white race,
> demands separate houses of worship.... If the
> Church would win them for Christ she must provide
> for them church-edifices of their own. Build
> houses for them, consecrate them and let them know
> they are for them and we will find little
> difficulty in gathering them in and blessing them
> for Christ. We can do this, of course, without
> making any race distinction or raising separate
> altars. They will still be part and parcel of the
> Church, in full communion with it and entitled to
> representation in the diocesan convention. [11]

Such reports are somewhat puzzling, for one would suppose
that the blacks would want to worship with the whites and be
fully accepted into the white Church. Apparently this was
not the case because the the blacks knew that they were not
really welcomed into the white churches. They wanted a
church building that they could call their own, so that they
could conduct their business in the manner they thought was
best. Independence and self-respect was just as important as

inclusion in the larger, white church.

There was another reason for this demand for separate churches: the blacks did not trust the Church's long-term commitment to them and to their problems. They believed the Church missionaries would be here one day and gone the next. The Rev. W.E. Webb at the Antrim Mission in Halifax, Virginia underscored this deep suspicion when he wrote to the Spirit of Missions in 1883:

> But, as a whole, they are afraid of our Church. They are not certain we desire them very much. They have an unutterable dread of being laughed at, for they feel their ignorance. They therefore like to be together, and to be in congregations by themselves. They are not certain that Missions or schools sustained at a distance (and we have not the means here as yet to sustain them) will be permanent. Then they must endure persecution from their own, if after a brief period these influences are withdrawn. [12]

Only a long and committed ministry could erase such a suspicion.

The Episcopal Church slowly realized that the demise of the Home Missions Committee was a mistake. The Domestic Missions department repeatedly said at its annual meetings that no new progress was being made in regard to its ministry to the blacks. Church officials started to take notice of this stalemate and they worried. They were concerned not just because the blacks were living in poverty and consequently should be helped, but also because they thought the health of the nation was endangered. They were afraid

that the plight of the blacks would propel the nation into a
decline, and they felt responsible. It was the Episcopal
Church, of all the churches, which could restore the health
of the nation. The Church had a mission to the blacks, as
well as all racial groups, because of national interests. The
Rev. William S. Langford, General Secretary of Domestic
Missions, said in his annual report in 1886 to the Board of
Managers:

> No person can contemplate the rapid growth of
> population, present and prospective, without
> feeling a serious concern as to what shall be the
> moral and social condition of new communities
> which are springing up, and as to what shall be
> the character of the nation which in the last half
> of the nineteenth century shall have doubled its
> population and become the wonder of the world.
> Upon this American Church rests in large part the
> responsibility for the moulding and shaping of the
> vigorous life of this nation. The Church must
> have a consciousness of her mission to bless the
> people of this land, and all her members should be
> aroused to a sense of duty to the times in which
> they are living. [13]

The Church had a definite ministry both to individuals and to
the nation as a whole. In order to fulfill its divine
mission, the Church had to be more serious and determined
about its missions to the black population. Accordingly, the
Church Commission for Work among Colored People was
established by General Convention in 1886. [14]

The question of a commission arose through the efforts
of two men from the Diocese of Maryland. The Rev. Calbraith
B. Perry petitioned the Convention to create a new body to

coordinate the Church's work among the blacks, and his petition was strongly supported by the Hon. J. C. Bancroft Davis of Maryland. [15] Other delegates supported these efforts, and a committee was formed to investigate the matter. The committee determined that the Church had failed to address the blacks' needs and that a commission should be established in Washington D.C. to oversee the Church's work. However, this commission could not dictate what actions would be taken to help the black people; this was left to the bishops of the individual dioceses.[16] Both houses approved the resolution and the Commission for Work among Colored People was born. Its membership consisted of five bishops, five presbyters and five laymen. [17]

This commission met for the first time on 19 and 20 January 1887, in Washington D.C., although it was not legally to come into existence until 1 September 1887. [18] The Chairman pro tempore was Bishop William Paret of Maryland; Mr. John Newton was the secretary pro tempore. Three goals were established by the Commission: "(1) Increase of diocesan appropriations. (2) Training of new workers, and at this time especially of well qualified Deacons, for immediate work. (3) The building of chapels and school houses." [18] These goals were intended to place the Church's ministry on a firm financial basis, provide real support to the blacks, and circumvent the many problems of finding both white and black presbyters to minister to the blacks.

The emphasis upon deacons meant that the church could employ people who wanted to minister to the blacks but who might not be able to do so as presbyters because they could not meet the stringent educational standards expected of the presbyters. Rigorous academic preparation for the presbyterate was the major stumbling block to interested black men who wanted to minister to their own people; the white standards were too demanding given the blacks limited educational opportunities. It was hoped that this emphasis upon deacons would allow more black men to minister to their own people. A "black" diaconate did not emerge because the Church wanted its black pastors to be highly educated. Intellectual clergy were a definite sign of the blacks blossoming redemption.

Sunday-schools, parish schools, normal schools, and theological schools were to be emphasized and established in those dioceses seeking to help the blacks. It was thought that by raising their level of education, the blacks then could begin to appreciate the great riches that the Church had to offer them, and consequently become better Christians and better citizens. The Commission for Work among Colored People's annual report to the Board of Missions in 1892 said in part:

> Schools are the opening wedge. The one point on which our missionaries and agents are unanimous is the need of additional schools, and the virtual impossibility of producing any permanent impression on the people without them. A good parochial school is the burden of each report.

One reads such words as, 'It is almost waste of money to plant a church and not have a school.' [20]

Such reports were received from the field because the many Church members believed that the salvation of the black race could only occur once they were educated. No education, no salvation; it was as simple as that. Such thinking was predicated upon the common assumptions that the many Americans held at this time. Whites within and without the Church were unsure as to how much the black race could learn. However, they did know one thing: the blacks were poorly educated, and the Episcopal Church intended to help them acquire the education that they needed to live and work in America.

The Commission encouraged the establishment of preparatory schools, industrial schools, and theological schools. The Commission itself authorized only one school (King Hall in Washington D.C.) to be opened; it was associated with Howard University. The Commission believed that the best results for theological training could be achieved if theological schools were formed alongside existing universities, thus providing the theological school with an expanded curriculum. This arrangement also benefited the university, as their students could attend classes at the theological school. This is exactly what happened at King Theological Hall.

This institution was founded in 1889 on property near Howard University. The money for the hall was given by the Hon. John A. King, and his generosity was rewarded by naming the institution in his honor. [21] Its first director was the Rev. Henry R. Pyne. [22] The school was successful in that it had a cordial relationship with Howard University, and it was incorporated by Congress in 1891. [23] Students were enrolled by 1891 and King Hall's rich history began. It soon became the preeminent theological school for black Episcopal students. Because of its success and because it was supported by the Commission for Work Among Colored People, other diocesan institutions that were responsible for preparing students for the ministry were asked to de-emphasize their theological training and to emphasize their preparatory or college education programs. This request arose because the Commission believed that there were too many theological schools for the number of black candidates and that the black candidates were more often than not ill-prepared for the rigors of theological education. The other Episcopal seminaries for blacks were St. Augustine's in Raleigh, North Carolina, Hoffman Hall in Nashville, Tennessee, and Payne Divinity School in Petersburg, Virginia. The Commission members hoped that by streamlining the system, the students would receive a better education and that the Church's money would be better utilized.

Efforts to improve the structure of the Church's

schools were partly successful. The trustees of St. Augustine's School agreed to concentrate its efforts on the preparatory phase of the students' education. Theological students were sent to King Hall by 1894. [24] This still left two other theological schools: Hoffman Hall, associated with Fiske University in Nashville, Tennessee, founded by the Diocese of Tennessee in 1890, and the Bishop Payne Divinity and Industrial School, founded in 1878 at Petersburg, Virginia. [25] The three schools served a very limited number of students. The Church did have a right to complain that there was duplication of services because three different institutions were serving probably no more than twenty or thirty students. But the larger question is why did separate institutions have to be established in the first place? The answer is clearly one of racial discrimination. Alexander Crummell sought admission to General Seminary in the 1839 and was denied admission because he was black. [26] General later changed its policy and did admit black students, but they were few in number. The Commission for Work among Colored People never considered sending every black student to a white school. There were veiled references to why more black students were not sent to General: that the climate was too cold or that it was too far away from their dioceses or that the social atmosphere in the North was too markedly different from that of the South. Yet no mention was ever made of sending candidates to the

Virginia Seminary, which was formed by southern dioceses for southern students. Indeed, King Hall and the Virginia Theological Seminary in Alexandria, Virginia were near to one another, even for nineteenth century modes of transportation.

There also was the belief that if black candidates for the ministry studied and trained for ministry with other black students, then they would be better prepared to minister to their own people. This indeed was partly true, but not totally. The curriculum in the black theological schools was basically the same as the white schools. It had to be, because the black students were to meet the same educational requirements as the whites. Consequently, the black clergy and even teachers were profoundly affected by the atmosphere of Church institutions and their middle-class values. One missionary in Georgia suggested that all schools for blacks should be established by buying property, building a school building, and erecting a home for the teacher. His reason highlights the fact that the Church's educational system not only educated but reinforced middle-class values:

> Colored teachers as well as our colored clergymen,
> who have been accustomed to the cleanliness and
> good cooking that may be noticed in the city homes
> of those who have been house-servants in
> well-to-do families, are unwilling, and in most
> cases refuse positively to board with the common
> field laborers even when they can offer them
> sleeping accommodation, and the white people, as a
> matter of course, will not receive them. [27]

This missionary believed the reason that the black school

teachers and clergymen were particular had to do just with the fact that they had been "house servants." The larger truth is that they had been middle "class-ized" by Church institutions.

If the students attending the theological schools were adapting to and even embracing middle-class values, one can ask why the students were not encouraged to attend white institutions. The clear fact is that the white membership of the Episcopal Church was no different than the average white person on the street: they did not want blacks in white schools because they looked upon the blacks as inferior. This attitude can be seen in an article written by Bishop Gailor of Tennessee in 1897 for a special issue of Spirit of Missions highlighting the Church's work among the blacks. He wrote:

> I have been asked to contribute to this number of THE SPIRIT OF MISSIONS my views on the subject of the work among the Colored people of the South--its necessity, its difficulties, its prospects. The first two points are answered almost in the very statement of them. The necessity is laid upon all our people, of every section, because we are all in our degree responsible for these 8,000,000 souls, who are here, through no fault of their own, as permanent factors in our government and civilization. The difficulties are apparent. The people are weak, childish, sensuous, improvident, without industry or self-control. Their religion, taken by and large, is an unmoral ecstasy, and political schemers have placed them in an attitude which the white people of the South regard as a menace to our social and political institutions. This is the necessity, these are the difficulties. The question for us to consider is: What practical policy can we inaugurate that shall in the long run yield the best results and lay the surest

> foundation for the ultimate regeneration of the
> Colored race...? ...To my mind there is one thing
> absolutely the most important, and at the same
> time practicable, and that is the creation of a
> class of men thoroughly willing and capable to
> lead and teach the people. What the Colored race
> needs to-day more than anything else is Colored
> men who can teach, who can lead, and who have the
> learning and character to be guides and examples
> of their race. [28]

We can can clearly see why the blacks were not welcomed into
white institutions and why the Church believed that only
blacks could fully and completely serve blacks. Certainly
the Anglo-Saxons did not consider themselves to be childish
or weak or sensuous; therefore, they could never really
understand the black race or its disposition. They needed
black men and women, trained in black schools, to serve the
black race.

Furthermore, it was believed that the blacks could not
just step into the white world and live and work as if they
had never been slaves. They had to earn the respect of the
white world by learning trades and proving that they were
capable of living up to the great freedoms of the United
States. Thus the Church entered into industrial schools,
schools that not only educated but provided the students with
skills to obtain a job and become contributing citizens of
society. Indeed, the Church was encouraged in its endeavors
by Booker T. Washington, who urged the Church to establish
industrial schools at all its missions:

> I cannot speak too highly of industrial training
> as part of the education needed by the Colored
> People. All education enlarges a man's wants. A
> mere literary training enlarges his wants without
> increasing his ability, outside of professional
> life, to meet them. A student comes to us, an
> ordinary field hand, earning thirty to fifty cents
> per day for a part of the year. While getting his
> education he learns a trade, and he goes out to
> find employment as a carpenter, a bricklayer, a
> tinner, or a dairyman, at from a dollar to two
> dollars per day. The same is true of the
> girls.... From these larger wants and these
> larger resources there soon comes the larger man
> and the better citizen. [29]

Booker T. Washington saw the industrial school as an

opportunity for the blacks to break into the white world by

learning skills that would boost their income and their

status in society.

While Mr. Washington saw the industrial school as an

opportunity, some within the Church saw it as a way also to

keep the black in his place. Such feelings were expressed

because some felt that the training of "the Negro race as we

would the white" would only bring discord between the two

races. [30] Instead, it was better to train the black

student so he would not produce friction among his white

counterparts, who were "1,400 years ahead of them in

development...." [31] Although the friction between the

races was a realistic concern, nonetheless we can see that it

was the black man or woman who was to make the compromises,

not the whites.

For both good and bad reasons, the Church quickly

embraced the idea of industrial schools and much good was
done through them. Such schools taught students masonry
skills, carpentry, sewing, nursing, and farming. The
students learned valuable skills and in turn the black
community was aided by gaining people who had talents that
were needed. One advocate of this program, Mrs. A. B. Hunter
of St. Augustine's School, Raleigh, North Carolina described
how she and many other Church members hoped such programs
would transform the black race; lift it above its uncultured
ways, to a new, more American lifestyle:

> The hundreds who have been raised by education are
> few compared with the great numbers of their race,
> and must lead a somewhat isolated life, above
> their own people, and on a different plane from
> the white man. We hope the time is not far
> distant when the numbers will be so increased that
> they can have their own stores, churches,
> institutions and cultured homes, and can work
> along their own lines as we work on ours, two
> races, side by side, friendly yet distinct. [32]

Mrs. Hunter's quaint hopes for the future did not
materialize, but nevertheless, remarkable progress was made.
Such industrial schools gave the students the opportunity to
better themselves, and instead of lifting the student above
their black counterparts, they brought enrichment to the
black society as a whole. The blacks could not escape from
their black world. No matter how much Mrs. Hunter may have
wanted a black, middle class society to emerge as the norm
for the black culture, there was little room for it. Black
graduates faced crises that affected the general black

population. Middle class ideals could not always function in the black world. There was neither the time nor the luxury for them. Missionaries, black and white, had very little money to buy necessary supplies whether they were for a school, church, or hospital. One hospital reported that it desperately needed a furnace to heat the hospital and that its patients were too poor to pay for care received. [33] A school teacher reported that her students were more on their knees than on their seats because they had to use their benches as desks. [34] Such conditions did not allow for middle-class ideals to flourish.

However, the Church was concerned about the level of education and morality among the blacks. Industrial schools were good to a point, but they did not reach a large section of the population. Accordingly, it was decided that the best way to aid the blacks was through the woman, wife, mother. It was the mother who, they supposed, had the most influence upon the entire family. It was she who cooked and nurtured the children; it was she who struggled to keep the family together and taught the children right and wrong. If the Church could win over the female, then the whole family could be converted to the Church. Accordingly, missionaries began instructing women and girls about the proper ways of doing housework, sewing, and cooking. One school teacher remarked about this work: "...we are doing all in our power to make of our girls whole-souled, clear-headed, pure-hearted Christian

women. They are to make our homes and our future race and no stream rises higher than its source." [35] Additionally, kindergartens were established, not only to serve a need for working mothers but also to bring mothers into contact with "mothers of the more refined and cultured class." [36]

This great effort to improve the moral character of the black race was not just a result of the Church wishing to bring more blacks into the fold. Some leaders felt it was their patriotic duty to help civilize this race. A great nation was founded upon the moral strength of families. Consequently, America could only be great if the blacks improved their morality. One woman explained why her bishop asked her to become a missionary to the blacks in Georgia:

> With the firm conviction that the family life is the true basis of a nation's greatness or degradation; that no nation rises higher than the people who compose it; that the people are what their homes make them; and that women are they who create the home atmosphere, the Bishop of Georgia sent me as a Bible-woman among the Negroes of Georgia. He sent me to try to find out the real conditions of their home life, in both city and country, and to study the best ways to help them upwards. [37]

More was at stake than just the membership roles of the Episcopal Church. The Church was on a messianic mission to save the entire country from ruin.

The blacks did not believe they needed any additional saving. They had their own ministers and their own churches, so they regarded the Church's attempts to minister to them

with suspicion and sometimes contempt. One missionary admitted that had he been a Baptist or Methodist the black people would have accepted him and his free school quickly and gratefully. The community church buildings would have been open for his use, but he was barred from the churches because he was an Episcopalian. The Baptist and Methodist ministers would not allow him to use their buildings. [38] The Episcopal Church had to enter the community without any support from the people. He asked for money to build a school and buy supplies because he knew it would take time to win the people over; they could, in fact, only be won if they saw the Church's commitment in brick and mortar and not in words and promises. The blacks had heard too many promises from the whites in the past, so they were not going to be duped again. Ministry to the blacks was not an easy affair for Episcopalians because of their own prejudice against the blacks and because the blacks tended to scorn the validity and significance of the Church's ministry and worship.

When the church was successful in its ministry, the blacks openly supported and welcomed the services that the church supplied. The missionary in the aforementioned paragraph, the Rev. H. Dunlop, of Ogeechee River Mission in Georgia, was not about to be driven from the community because of suspicion and prejudice. He stayed. His ministry slowly grew, and he was accepted into the community. He became ill and was taken to Savannah for treatment. Rumor

spread through the black community that he was not receiving proper treatment at the hospital. A large group of people from his congregation walked to Savannah and demanded to know, "at the hospital door," the condition of their parson. Verbal assurances were not enough for them. They refused to leave "until a small committee had been allowed to see 'the pahson' in the room and learn from him that 'it was all right' and that he was in good and safe hands." [39] This anecdote illustrates the great love that the blacks had for this minister and their deep acceptance of the Episcopal Church because of this man's efforts. It also illustrates how unsure the blacks were of their position within the society and the Church. They could not believe the parson was being treated properly because they themselves were not treated properly by the society. Since he ministered to them, the outcasts of Church and society, they assumed he would be devalued and not given proper medical treatment. The bishop of Georgia told this story as an example of the blacks deep and lasting "fidelity." [40] Beneath this fidelity, however, lay a deep and overwhelming suspicion that the white church and culture would take away whatever "good" they had in their lives. The visitation of the parson was more a matter of looking after their own interests than it was a sign of fidelity.

This loyalty to the Episcopal Church was not an isolated incident. Once the Church established itself within

the community and demonstrated its concern, it usually attracted a committed and dedicated congregation. There is even one instance when a black, non-Episcopal congregation petitioned to join the diocese of North Carolina. The petition was unexpected, and the diocese was quite surprised. This congregation belonged to the African Methodist Episcopal Zion denomination, but had, for some unmentioned reason, become disgruntled. [41] A small delegation was sent to the black congregation, and the delegation discovered that the congregation was determined to leave the former denomination and join the Episcopal Church. Officials of the African Methodist Episcopal Zion denomination heard of the planned departure from the fold, so they sent a representative to meet with the congregation and the Episcopal delegation. He asked that the Episcopal Church cease interfering with the affairs of the conference. Apparently it was an amicable meeting in which both sides showed great sensitivity to one another. The Episcopal delegates refused to hold a service in the church, as requested by the trustees, because a service had already been scheduled by the official denomination. Instead, they held a service at time which would not interfere with the regularly scheduled service. [42] The congregation eventually joined the Episcopal Church. This incident demonstrates that the Episcopal Church was not necessarily an alien force within the life of the black community. When sincere interest, sensitivity, and

honesty was employed by the Church among the black people, it could indeed have an effective and important ministry.

Such ministry was largely based upon the attitude of the missionary or school teacher. He or she was the one who came into direct contact with the blacks and established the level of rapport that developed between the church/school and the community. In most instances, the missionaries were sensitive to the needs of the black community. Even when we might question their motives and see that the reason for their ministry was based more upon racial fear than upon a deep, abiding interest in the welfare of the people, the ministry was usually effective and welcome. It was welcomed because most of the blacks were poor and needed any help they could get. It was accepted because, beneath the layers of prejudice, there was a great deal of human love, love that even the missionary found hard to explain and perhaps to accept. Letter after letter was sent to the Spirit of Missions illustrating the great needs of the missionaries. Often the letters were nothing more than a report with statistics and pithy comments. Other times, the letters were pregnant with emotion and concern for the black people. One outstanding letter was sent to the Spirit of Missions by the missioner at Wilmington, North Carolina in 1889:

> I have, I may say, some five hundred souls under
> my care. More than otherwise. These include all
> sorts and conditions, from the poverty-stricken to
> the comparatively well-to-do. Of these latter I
> have four, perchance five families; all the
> others are poor, poorer, poorest. Some I clothe

almost entirely, and others I feed. One man told
my wife that all he and his had to eat this winter
was what I had given them. I have to buy medicine
for the sick, bury the dead, warm the cold and
clothe the naked, besides making the repairs on
the school that are absolutely necessary. It
keeps me poor and continually hard up. But what
am I to do? I cannot sit by the bedside of a poor
dying woman, as I did the other day, and say in
answer to her pleading, dying looks, 'Be thou
clothed, be thou warmed.' No, I can only say,
'Here is an order for a load of wood.' To tell of
one case out of many, that woman died in my arms,
as I raised her from the pillow to give her the
Holy Communion. I laid her back, finished the
service, and left the shrieking children with
their dead mother, to be consoled by their
relatives and friends. I was exhausted, and it was
hard to keep the tears back and control my
trembling body. [43]

While the missionary among the blacks was struggling to

meet the many needs of the people, the Commission for Work

Among Colored People also found itself struggling to cope

with the expectations of the missionaries, bishops, and the

Foreign and Domestic Missionary Society of the Episcopal

Church. The Commission's origins were troubled from the very

beginning. It had to work with too little money and too many

members with varied opinions. Five bishops, five presbyters,

and five laymen, from the north and south, comprised its

membership. [44] Disagreements arose among this diverse group

as to how the Commission's work should be conducted. In any

case, the Commission could do little more than focus the

Church's attention upon its programs for the blacks. The

very constitution of the Commission forbade it to interfere

with the will and desire of the diocesan bishops within whose jurisdictions the ministry was taking place. [45] The diocesan bishops chose the missionaries who worked in their dioceses and oversaw their work. The Commission officially approved the selection of the diocesan missionaries and determined whether national Church funds were available to pay for the missionary's salary and expenses. It was powerful only in the awarding or the withholding of funds for specific missionary work. This august body was little more than a clearing house for money.

Even in the financial realm the Commission lacked power to prepare a budget and then receive the level of funding needed to finance its programs. Its budget was set by the Board of Managers of the Domestic and Missionary Society of the Episcopal Church. In its first year of work, the Board of Managers allocated to the Commission only $12,000.00 plus all designated money that the Board received for work among the blacks. [46] This designated money was not of a considerable amount. On 11 June 1889 the Board of Managers reported that $12,396.43 had been received for work among the blacks. [47] There was not enough money to go to the different missionary endeavors. As a result everyone was dissatisfied. The Commission knew that it did not have enough money and kept insisting that it needed more. Its pleadings did move the Board of Managers to issue it more funds, although this was a gradual process. In 1896, the

Board of Missions passed a resolution instructing the Board of Managers to make an appropriation of $70,000 to the Commission for Work Among Colored People. However, when the Board of Managers tried to increase the allocation, they found they did not have the resources to do so. If they increased the Commission's funding, then some other program would have to be cut. The Board of Managers was not willing to risk this move, probably because of political reasons and probably because they did not think that such an increase was necessary, especially if it were to deprive other valued programs of needed funding. It appears that the appropriations for the Commissions work never did rise beyond $62,000. [48]

This lack of money was always a problem for the Commission. A General Appeal Letter was sent to parishes across the country by the Commission's General Agent, Bishop C.C. Penick. He said of the Commission's financial crisis: "I appeal to every communicant entrusted with means, by the compassion of Him 'who for our sakes became poor,' to give as largely and promptly as possible. I appeal to the poor in purse, but rich in grace, to send at once some help, be it ever so small and follow it with your prayers. The crisis is sharp, the need urgent." [49]

Bishop Penick's position as General Agent for the Commission was created in 1893 to arouse interest among the parishes and to gain an increase in contributions. [50] This

job was demanding and exhausting. Between 1893 and 1896 he addressed coventions in thirteen different dioceses, preached 450 times, prepared pamphlets, and authored a series of eight papers explaining the Church's relationship with the blacks. These papers were sent to every congregation with 100 or more parishioners. [51] The reaction to Bishop Penick's appeals was minimal. An editorial in the Spirit of Missions in 1896 lamented: "...ears are deaf and hearts are cold, and the work, which has been well done, so far as the means in hand would permit, is suffered to languish when it should be supplied with money enough to make it grow and flourish." [52] People inside and out of the Commission began to question whether the General Agent's position was necessary. The money spent for his salary was needed for other, more important items. Bishop Penick resigned his position by October 22, 1896. [53] The implication was clear: the average church member was not interested in giving money to aid the Church's work among the black people.

Despite financial hardships, the Commission valiantly struggled to serve the black community. The Missionary Council of the Domestic and Foreign Missionary Society reported in 1896 that there were 146 church and school buildings serving the blacks. Academic schools and industrial schools were open in Raleigh, North Carolina; Lawrenceville, Virginia; Petersburg, Virginia; Washington, D.C.; and Nashville, Tennessee. In addition there were many smaller

schools throughout the South. [54] Over 4,346 students were enrolled in all the schools. [55] There were also 7,116 communicants in the missionary congregations. [56]

Time and time again requests were submitted to the Commission which could not be honored because the Commission did not have the money. It was very reluctant to withdraw money from any established center until the mission was self-sufficient. This attitude probably reflected a profound concern for the mission they helped to create and the knowledge that mission's bishop would be extremely disturbed by the withdrawal of funds. Bishop Satterlee of Washington D.C. reported that the following happened when the Commission tried to change diocesan appropriations:

> ...At the last meeting at which Bishop Dudley was
> present, a strong effort was made to cut down and
> change appropriations, because some Dioceses
> seemed to be doing more active work than others.
> After the meeting adjourne (sic) such
> representations were made to Bishop Dudley, from
> the Dioceses whose appropriations were thus cut
> down, that we went back to the old schedule. [57]

The Commission toyed with the idea picked up from the African Methodist Episcopal Church to gradually withdraw financial support from missions forcing them to become self-supporting. They also tried to link missions with private persons, congregations, or auxiliary groups who could support the mission, thus providing the mission with needed funds and encouraging the benefactor to take a personal interest in the mission. [58] Neither approach was very

effective, probably because of the great poverty of the missions and the lack of interest on the part of the larger Church. Also, why should the mission congregations want to make large financial sacrifices to join a larger church body that was so suspicious of them? Very few black people wanted to give time and money to an organization which viewed them as second-class citizens.

Just as the Commission struggled with financial problems, it also struggled with structural problems. The Commission was too unwieldy and its members came from many different areas of the country. Many members had a difficult time attending all the meetings. The meetings were usually held in Washington D.C. once a month, and usually only people from the surrounding area could attend the meetings. The Commission's secretary, in a letter to the Rev. Dr. Langford, General Secretary of the Domestic and Foreign Missionary Society, said that the Commission did not have regular attendance; there were never more than eleven people. [59] He suggested that more members might be able to attend the meetings if they were held in New York City at the Church Missions House. [60]

By 1895, the Commission had yet to have one black member elected to its membership. This was true despite repeated requests sent to the Domestic and Foreign Missionary Society by the Colored Workers Conferences for black representation on the Commission. [61] Finally, in 1896, the

Rev. Dr. Alexander Crummell, a black priest, was confirmed by the Board of Missions and took his seat on the Commission for Work Among Colored People. [62] It is interesting that the secretary of the Commission had to remind the General Secretary of the Domestic and Foreign Mission Society that the black people had asked for representation on the Commission for several years. It demonstrates how powerless the Commission was to control its own destiny and highlights the apathy that the general Church felt toward the black race and their status in society. [63] The Board of Managers only acted when the Commission for Work Among Colored People continued to pressure it. It is certain that the Board would not have appointed a black member without such urging. Apparently they were afraid of the message of the black's equality that this action would send to the Church, especially to their southern members.

The division between the North and the South was apparent from the very beginning of the Commission. The work of the Church only took place within the former slave states, although blacks lived in all parts of the country and the Commission was asked by some bishops outside of the old slave states to help them in their ministry. They were always refused. The southern bishops were suspicious of this national Church agency which was to oversee the work that took place in their dioceses with their missionaries. They wanted the funding, but they certainly did not want outside

help, especially from northerners. This division between north and south, and the lingering suspicion by the southern bishops that the Commission might try to interfere with diocesan policy, further weakened the Commission.

Bishop Dudley was aware of the Commission's ineffectiveness and in 1889 formed a special committee to formulate structural changes that would increase the Commission's impact. The committee recommended that the Commission's membership come only from those dioceses in which the Commission's work was taking place, that a Missionary Bishop for blacks be elected, and that the Commission have exclusive jurisdiction over the ministry to the blacks. [64] These recommendations were never approved by the Commission for Work among Colored People because they were too controversial. Although dioceses still had the privilege of deciding whether to become a part of the Commission and could leave at any time, the recommendations removed the jurisdiction of the blacks from the diocesan bishops' hands and gave this power to the Commission. The bishops could not agree to such a proposal, even though the Commission was to be run directly by the southern bishops, clergy, and laity. Sovereign dioceses did not want their rights to be jeopardized by any national commission, even a commission directly controlled by their own constituents.

The aforementioned suggestion that missionary bishops for the black people be established was becoming a popular

thought among some church leaders. Such bishops were wanted in order to increase the Commission's power and efficiency as well as to appeal to the black people. The Missionary Council in 1891 requested that the General Convention take action creating such an office. This bishop would have "territorial jurisdiction but without interfering with any present diocesan authority." [65] Probably this request was influenced by the existence of bishops for the American Indians; a bishop had been sent to minister to the Indian people in 1873 [66] This act changed the manner in which the Church saw its bishops. Prior to 1873, bishops always ministered in a specific geographical area to all the people in that area. The sending of a special bishop who was to work only with the Indians sent a clear message to the whole Church. Not only could bishops serve specific territorial regions, but they could also serve specific races of people. It made sense, to many church members, that bishops for the black people would be beneficial to the Church and to the black people.

At the General Convention of 1889, Mr. Wilmer of Maryland presented a proposed canon that would have created special missionary districts for blacks, thus allowing the blacks to have their own bishops. [67] The Committee on Canons opposed the creation of separate bishops for blacks and in part said:

This Canon proposes an Episcopal jurisdiction 'in personas' within the territorial jurisdiction of

another Bishop. We think that such a proposition
antagonizes the history and traditional policy of
the Church, and the essential elements of
Episcopal jurisdiction which, from the first, has
been territorial and not personal.
   But the real and essential question which meets
us at the forefront of the whole matter, and which
we think the Church should first determine...is
that first alluded to in this report, namely:
Shall the Church, in its law of parochial or
diocesan organizations, draw or recognize a line
of distinction between its white and its colored
members? We think this should not be done....[68]

The essential question was raised by this committee, and the

General Convention agreed with the answer: no special bishops

for the blacks.

We cannot definitely know why this convention refused

to create special bishops. However, the delegates probably

sensed that the establishment of special bishops would

overtly recognize the unspoken division that separated the

two races within the Church. White Episcopalians were

reluctant to widen the division. Black Episcopalians did not

support such a move because they wanted equality, not

separation. While this same Convention of 1889 was in

session, a special memorial was presented by the Conference

of Colored Clergy and other Workers of the Church among

Colored People. The memorial was in reaction to two dioceses

refusing to seat black delegates at their diocesan

conventions. The memorial asked: "Is it in accordance with

the real doctrines taught by this Church, that when men have

once been admitted to the Sacred Ministry or that when men

have once been admitted to the Sacred Ministry or Communion of the Church any restriction should be made in the spiritual or legislative rights of a colored man which would not be made in those of a white man?" [69] The actions of these dioceses and the memorial itself embarrassed the Convention. A reply was written in response to the memorial which said: "...This General Convention has by no act or law admitted or implied that a difference of race or color affords ground for a distinction in legislative rights or privileges." [70] The fabric of this Holy, Catholic, and Apostolic Church remained unblemished and whole. Racial differences were not recognized before God or the General Convention of the Episcopal Church.

The movement to create a missionary bishop for the blacks died, but the realization that more efficient organization was needed remained. The position of Archdeacon for Colored Work was created. This person was appointed by the local bishop and worked only among the black people. The position of "archdeacon" seemed to satisfy both the whites and the blacks, since the blacks were better served and the bishops remained firmly in control of what happened within their own dioceses.

Although the establishment of Archdeacons enabled diocesan work to proceed more smoothly, there were still lingering doubts that the Commission for Work Among Colored People was actually needed. Bishop William Paret of

Maryland, a member of the Commission since its conception, wrote to the General Secretary of the Domestic and Foreign Missions Society to express his concerns about the necessity for the Commission:

> For my own part I am coming to feel that the work for the Colored people can be quite as effectively managed by the managers sitting in New York as it can by the present Commission. I think that the Commission has been very effective and helpful and has accomplished a great deal, and that if the work can now be transferred retaining the sympathy and strength which has been gained, it would be better. Our bishops and Clergy who compose the Commission are widely scattered, too much so for very effective action. [71]

Bishop Paret also relayed to Dr. Langford the suspicion, that members of the Commission had, that he was not sympathetic to the Commission's work. The Bishop was clearly disturbed about the inefficiency of the Commission but also illustrated the Commission's fear that, if it were dissolved, the work would not be done. This was a genuine concern because since this was exactly what happened when the Home Missions for Colored Peoples was dissolved in 1878.

We can see from this letter that people were questioning the role of the Commission. For some the Commission was a necessary evil; it was inefficient, powerless, and, indecisive, yet it still focused, although weakly, the Church's attention on the problem of the blacks. It was better to offer the black community some succor than no succor at all. But not all agreed with this philosophy.

Some, especially the southern Bishops, felt that the Commission was not firm enough in handling the black situation. Their dissatisfaction with the Commission can be seen in their reaction to the Commission's only officially established institution, the aforementioned King Hall. As we shall soon see, the southern bishops stopped sending their candidates for ordination to King Hall.

Bishop Satterlee of Washington D.C., in a letter to Bishop Greer, the new chairman of the committee to oversee the Church's ministry to the blacks when the Commission for Work among Colored People was dissolved in 1904, told Greer of the controversy surrounding King Hall. It centered on W. V. Tunnell, a black priest and the Warden of King Hall, and on a undefined scandal which saw two students expelled and the rest suspended for one year. Bishop Satterlee saw Mr. Tunnell as a "'bumptious'" man who "offended everyone, and especially Southerners, by his conceited, consequential and patronising manner." [72] Apparently this scandal and Mr. Tunnell's personality was enough to make the "Southern Bishops...lose all sympathy with King Hall." [73] The end result was that they would not send their students to King Hall. All the students were from "Connecticut, Pennsylvania, Vermont and other Northern Dioceses, and also some West Indians." [74] One trustee of King Hall, Dr. McKim, suggested that King Hall consider moving to Southern Virginia to merge with Bishop Payne Divinity School. [75] One Bishop

even suggested to the Commission that King Hall be closed since Washington D.C. "was not the place in which the right kind of colored ministry could be educated." [76]

The issue here was not one of education but of prejudice and control. The southern bishops were afraid of any institution (that was not directly under their authority) that educated men for ministry. Regional seminaries were part of the Episcopal Church's polity, and therefore the bishops especially did not want their black candidates to be educated in a seminary that was beyond their control and was perhaps too liberal for their taste. King Hall had the best facilities of all the seminaries for blacks to provide the black candidates with an excellent education. But the bishops were frightened by the institution because they did not directly regulate its policies and curriculum and therefore could not directly control the students. They wanted their candidates for the ordained ministry educated, but they did not want them to be influenced by thoughts and ideas that were not in keeping with the mores of Southern culture. Even the location of the seminary in Washington D.C. probably frightened, them because at least one third of the population was black. [77] To have their students living in an area with many black people and attending a seminary controlled by the Commission was just too risky for them. King Hall's problems were not extreme. The Bishops were looking for an excuse not to send their students to King

Hall, and they capitalized on the faults that were uncovered.

Such criticisms of the Commission ate away at its longevity. The General Convention in 1904 dissolved the Commission and created a committee under the direction of the Board of Managers of the Domestic and Foreign Missions Society. [78] The Commission died as quickly and as silently as it was born. Just before the General Convention, the Commission met and did not discuss its approaching demise. Its members must have known that the end of the Commission was near, although the thought of this probably did not distress too many of the them. The Church's work would continue because the bishops would fight for their appropriations for black ministry. The bishops were the ones who made the decisions. The Rev. Mr. Tunnell, warden of King Hall, prophesied that the Commission was destined to fail. Indeed, it was really created to fail. He said in 1898, some six years before its dissolution:

> ...The Commission has not been free to develop along the lines of perceived needs and opportunities. It has had no control over or even direction of anything to whose being or well-being it has been the financial mainstay. It has been powerless to adopt and pursue a vigorous missionary policy or to initiate methods to give form and effect to its best wisdom and experience. It has scarcely an advisory authority.... In short, the Commission is little more than a bureau of information, appeal, and apportionment, and there its rights, duties, and functions have ended. Its purpose is a useful one, but one which quite effectually prevents if from becoming a vigorous and aggressive missionary agency. [79]

No one mourned the death of such a weak and powerless commission.

Through a Mirror Dimly

Neither the North nor the South ever dreamed that the rockets fired at Fort Sumter would set off a staggering explosion that would rock all of the United States. The explosion was not just about armed forces, fighting, victory, and defeat; it was about conflicting ideas that determined whether personal freedom would be granted to every citizen, despite racial characteristics. The Civil War was really a revolutionary war, for it provided the country with new revolutionary freedoms and ideas: all United States citizens became legally equal and had the right to pursue personal liberty and happiness. No longer were such liberties reserved for the ruling white class; they were extended to the blacks as well. The physical wound of division was healed by the victory of the Union troops, but a much deeper racial division remained. How could the whites and blacks live together in peace and harmony?

This question disturbed every white citizen. No matter whether the person had been an abolitionist or a supporter of slavery, the freeing of the slaves made former debates moot and raised a new, troubling thought: Could the black people live responsible lives as a freed people? Many whites doubted that this could ever happen without substantial help

from the white race. Societies were formed, public and private, to aid the black people in adjusting to freedom by providing them with food, clothing, and education.

The Episcopal Church sensed that it needed to assist the freedmen in order to help heal the country, so at its General Convention in 1865, it established the Protestant Episcopal Freedman's Commission or the Home Missions Commission for Colored People. [1] This Commission existed until 1877 when the General Convention determined that this work could be consolidated with its domestic missions department in the Domestic and Foreign Missionary Society. Work among the blacks was managed by this department for ten years until the General Convention once again determined that a special commission was needed. In 1887 the Commission for Work Among Colored People was born;it existed until 1904 when its responsibilities were once again given to the domestic missions department. [2]

The vacillation by General Convention in regard to its support of the two commissions reflected the uncertainties that the Church and society had about their efforts to assist the blacks. They were willing to give help and realized that their assistance was beneficial to the black people, but significant doubt loomed over their support of such efforts. Racial prejudice, sometimes subtly and other times boldly, whispered that the blacks did not need any help. Their problems were caused by their own inferiority. If the whites

just left them alone, the blacks would stay in their own separate world: content, happy, and childlike.

Probably the General Conventions would have been content to accept such reasoning, had not its own theology and images of itself prodded this blissful giant into acting on behalf of the black people. The convention understood itself to be a "Catholic" church, including all and excluding no one. All races, peoples, tongues, and nations had a home in the Church with apostolic succession and a rich catholic heritage that began with Jesus' birth in a poor stable in Bethlehem. So when its own delegates reminded the convention of its catholic tradition and urged it to help the black people, the convention acted. Commissions were formed that really did help the black people: thousands of blacks were educated, clothed, fed, and evangelized. The problem was that the Convention, bishops, presbyters, and laity did not truly want to help the black people. They could respond to prophetic calls for help but they could not become that prophetic voice which could stir the Church and the nation to dedicated and sincere actions that might have changed the face of the Church and the Country. They were ensnarled in a net of racial prejudice.

The black people sensed this lack of enthusiasm and so rejected the Church's invitation to become members. They could accept the Church's help but could not bring themselves to join an organization that discriminated against them. [3]

They demanded freeing, uplifting religious experiences because such services validated their heritage and allowed them to escape from earthly oppression with heavenly rapture. Thus, blacks naturally sought out church groups which validated their blackness and gave them courage to face daily oppressive discrimination. Often these church groups were entirely black, because it was only in the comfort and the support of their own race that they could truly live in freedom. Within their own churches, the blacks could experience God using their own expectations and cultural expressions. No one would tell them that their trances, visions, or conversion experiences were superstitious and barbaric. Through such religious phenomenon they sought God and their cultural roots. Their God was not just the white Christian God; He was the God who had lived with them in Africa before the Anglo-Saxons upset their world.

The majority of the Episcopal leadership and Commission agents could not understand that the black people had a valid cultural background that was radically different from the Anglo-Saxon heritage. This majority constantly tried to make the black people over in the white race's image because little of value was found within the traditions of the black race. It was a bastardization, a mutation that the white race had a responsibilities to correct, thus making it good, holy, pure, and moral. [4] This explains why the Church sent out teachers to aid the blacks. It was only through

education that the blacks could begin to appreciate the superior values held by the white race and those of the Episcopal Church. Such a view was held by Bishop C.C. Penick who served for five years as a bishop in West Africa and who was the general agent of the Church Commission for Work Among Colored People. [5] Despite his many years of work among the black people, his racist opinions did not weaken, and he believed that the blacks were inferior and could not associate with the whites until they overcame this inferior nature. [6] He and other officials within the Church thought that if the blacks could not change their skin color, at least the Church and society could make them adhere to Anglo-Saxon values, for only these values could redeem them before God and society.

Such perceptions explain why the General Conventions never considered modifying its academic requirements for black men seeking ordination or its stringent rules concerning the use of its Book of Common Prayer. The Church thought it was really doing the blacks a favor by making them adhere to the superior, white standards. Thus, it might have fewer black clergy and members because of its standards, but these blacks at least would have made the effort to improve on their poor, black heritage. The Church also could not think about amending its rubrics concerning the use of the Prayer Book because this book uplifted the blacks. To become Episcopalians meant that the blacks had to try to become like

white Episcopalians and forget their own cultural heritage.
In this respect the Church was egalitarian, in that there
were no distinctions between white and black: every candidate
seeking ordination fulfilled the same educational
requirements and all church members worshipped in the same
manner. However, such requirements devalued the differences
that existed between the two worlds, gave no credence to
black traditions, and forbade any black differences to
emerge. In attempting to be uniform, the Church had placed
its black members in straight-jackets.

The General Convention did not represent every
viewpoint within the Episcopal Church. Church members
answered the Church's call to service and valiantly attempted
to serve the black race's needs. Some of these missionaries
did not realize that the General Convention created these
commissions hoping that the black race and its problems would
disappear. Others who knew did not care why the commissions
were formed; they were only interested in serving the needs
of the black people. This explains why credible work was
achieved in a sea of cynicism and why Commission members and
teachers worked so hard to make the Commission's work
successful. [7] They were answering a deeper, spiritual call
that bade them to work among the blacks. Many of these
teachers and missionaries discriminated against the blacks in
various ways, and many could not appreciate the blacks' need
to have emotional worship services, but in spite of these

obstacles respect grew and a great desire burned in the agents' souls; they wanted to save the blacks in the name of Jesus of Christ. [8]

It was the personal faith of this minority that saved the program created by the majority from complete and utter failure. Such faith allowed the first treasurer of the Home Missions Commission to stand for hours waiting to buy surplus government clothes to be sent to the blacks, and it allowed teachers to talk about their black students with pride and exclaim that they could learn just as well as white students. [9] Failures and internal Church politics did not diminish their interest. This mission was important to these people because they believe it was central to the life and mission of the Episcopal Church. The Rev. John M. Pollard, Archdeacon for Colored Work in North Carolina, exuded this feeling when he exclaimed:

> I have given much thought to this question of work
> among the colored people and I have not yet felt
> convinced any further separation than we now have
> would lead to any better results. The unity of the
> Church of God is of far more vital importance than
> any temporary expediency....
> When I stand up and say: 'I believe in the Holy
> Catholic Church; the Communion of Saints:' I mean
> it. And when I pray, in that incomparable Litany:
> 'That it may please Thee to bless and keep all Thy
> people. That it May please Thee to bring into the
> way of truth all such as have erred and are
> deceived.' I mean it and have no apology to offer
> for my declaration of belief as stated in the
> Creed or my prayers as uttered in the Litany.
> They come from the very depths of my nature. [10]

These missionaries were not just missionaries of the

Commissions or the diocese; they were agents of God.

They were, as well, changed people. Their contact with the black people was the catalyst for a profound metamorphosis: their racial discrimination turned into respect. Such transformations are seen in the missionary who pleaded for the Church to truly accept the black people as equals and to end its prejudice; it is seen in the quaint hopes of a woman that the black people might be able to live side by side whites, all cloaked in the warmth of middle-class values. [11] We find it among the tears of the priest who ministered to the dying black woman in the midst of the squalor of poverty. [12] The black people became more than stereotypes for the white teachers and missionaries; they became brothers and sisters in faith, living human beings with hopes, dreams, and desires.

Seeing the blacks with new eyes enabled the missionaries to become advocates for the blacks within the larger, uncaring Church. The agents sensed the fickle nature of the General Convention and bishops, and they knew that these groups supported their programs partly out of fear and guilt. But their letters to the Spirit of Missions and to the Domestic and Foreign Missionary Society reminded the officials, over and over again, that the blacks desperately needed the hope and love of the Church. They became the courageous, prophetic voices calling the community of the faithful into a new relationship with God and its neighbors.

Often the Church turned a deaf ear, but the Commission's agents never gave up. They had an important ministry, and they were not about to desert the black people.

The blacks were affected by the dedication of these Episcopal agents. They at first held them at bay, suspicious of their motives. [13] But with time and devoted ministry, the blacks saw that some of these missionaries really cared about them as people. This care was demonstrated in the schools, churches, hospitals, and colleges opened for the black people. The blacks accepted this help, and, more importantly, began to accept the missionary as a friend, brother, and sister. Nowhere was this more poignantly demonstrated than when concerned black parishioners walked to the hospital where their white pastor was being treated. [14] They wanted to ensure that their pastor was being respected and given good medical care. The pastor and the parishioners touched one another and racial stereotypes were shattered.

In the end, it was the Gospel which had a profound effect upon the whites and the blacks. The Gospel moved a minority within the Episcopal Church to work among the black people with respect and love. Their faithful actions brought black people within the Church and forced the larger, white Church to examine its motives and conscience. I believe the best Biblical passage to describe what happen through these national commissions can be found in Paul's letter to the Corinthians. St. Paul talks about the spiritual gifts, and

then talks about love, the most mysterious and powerful of all the gifts. He says: "For now we see in a mirror dimly, but then face to face. Now I know in part; then I shall understand fully, even as I have been understood fully. So faith, hope, love abide, these three; but the greatest of these is love." [15] The Episcopal Church saw through a mirror dimly. It knew it was supposed to love the black race, yet never fully understood why or how. Still, it loved, projecting upon the race all its prejudices and stereotypes. Only as it grew in its understanding of itself and of the black people did its love increase and did it see more clearly. This love sometimes crushed and hurt; other times it uplifted and encouraged. But these first glimmers of love and help enabled the Church to open itself to a whole new race of people and a whole new world. It is far better for having done so. These first attempts to be more accepting of other races allowed the Episcopal Church to understand that it could only be a Holy Catholic Church if it it truly embraced all races of people in the name of Jesus Christ.

APPENDIX 1

Bylaws of the Executive Committee

I

Meetings of the Executive Committee

The stated meetings of the Executive Committee shall be held on the Thursday after the third Sunday in each month, at 1 o'clock, P.M.

Special meetings may be called by the Chairman at any time & shall be called by him at the written request of any two members. In the absence of the Chairman they may be called by two members - (No business shall be transacted at any special meeting save that which is specified in the call of the meeting -

II

1. The Corresponding Secretary
    The Corresponding Secretary shall conduct the general correspondence of the Commission & make a report at each stated meeting of the committee

2nd. The Treasurer
    The Treasurer shall report the state of the Funds at every meeting of the Committee & present a full & detailed report at the close of each fiscal year-

3rd. The Gen'l Agent
    The General Agent shall be in charge of the office of the Commissions, conduct its general business correspondence, & except in Dioceses where local & special Agents may be appointed, be charged with the duty of presenting the objects & claims of the Commission & of raising funds for the Treasury-- He shall be a member of each of the Sub Committees & their Secretary as well as the Secretary of the Executive Committee. He shall receive all applications & testimonials of persons desirous of becoming Teachers & all reports of Teachers & all applications for relief, & lay them before the appropriate Sub Committee-- He shall also render such Editorial Services as may be designated from time to time by the Executive Committee, on connection with the Spirit of Missions-- He shall make a full report of his acts at every stated meetings of the Executive Committee, accompanied with such recommendations of plans of operations as he may think expedient--

III

Sub Committees

There shall be three Sub Committees-- viz: on Teachers &
Schools, on Supplies & Relief, & on Finance; to be appointed
annually--
(1) The Sub Committee on Teachers & Schools shall consist of
five members-- This Sub Committee shall examine all
applications & testimonials of candidates for the post of
Teachers; recommend such as they may approve to the Executive
Committee for appointment, reporting the amount of Salary &
outfit which they may deem proper; select the necessary School
Books & apparatus; make such distribution thereof as they may
deem best; prepare instructions for the Teachers; consider &
report upon all questions of expenditure for rent of School
rooms, & outlay for supplies; examine the Reports of the
Teachers & in general exercise an oversight over the
Educational Department of the Committee work--

The Sub Committee on Supplies & Relief shall consist of Five
Members; & shall be charged with the receipt & distribution of
clothing & other necessaries for the relief of the Freedmen,
especially for the clothing of those who may desire to attend
our Schools. They shall examine all applications for
clothing & necessaries and report thereon at every meeting of
the Executive Committee-- In the recess of the com: they may
in urgent cases make such distribution of Supplies on hand as
they may deem expedient, & report the same at the next
meeting--

The Sub Committee on Finance shall consist of Three Members,
of whom the Treasurer shall be one, shall have charge of all
matters relating to the expenditure of money, They shall make
a Quarterly Report of all the liabilities of the Committee &
of the means of meeting the same accompanied with such
suggestions as they may deem expedient--
A majority of the members of each of these Sub Committees
shall constitute a quorum

ORDER OF BUSINESS

The following shall be the order of Business at each meeting--
(1) Reading of the minutes of the last meeting--
(2) Communications from the Chairman--
     Report of the Corresponding Secretary--
     "   " of the General Agent--
     "   " of the Sub Committees--
             On Teachers & Schools
             On Supplies & Relief
             On Finance
                  Special Committee--
     Notices & Resolutions growing out of the preceding
     communications & Reports in their order--

(Freedman's Aid Commission, Executive Minutes Book, 1865-1878,
Archives of the Episcopal Church, RG 41-55)

APPENDIX 2

The original members of the Freedman's Commission were: the Rt. Rev. Bishops Williams, Potter, Odenheimer, Stevens; Rev. Drs. Dix, A.H. Vinton, Hawks, E. Washburne, Littlejohn, Haight, Montgomery, Dyer; Rev. Edward Anthon, Rev. Drs. Diller, Eccleston, Howland; Messrs. H. Fish, Ruggles, F.S. Winston, John Welsh, John Bohlen, George D. Morgan, Robert B. Minturn, George C. Collins, John H. Swift, Stewart Brown, W.H. Aspinwall, John Travers. Added were: the Rev. Dr. Wharton and Huntington, and the Rev. John A. Aspinwall.

Recording Secretary - The Rev. John A. Aspinwall
Corresponding Secretary - The Rev. Dr. Wharton
Treasurer - Mr. Robert B. Minturn, Esq.; Mr. Minturn died and Mr. Stewart Brown, Esq. was elected.
Executive Committee: Haight, Vinton, Littlejohn, Eccleston, Fish, Winston, Morgan, and Welsh.

(Board of Missions, 1866, pp. 63-64.)

APPENDIX 3

Home Missions Commission's Objectives
1866

In entering upon their direct work, the committee, upon due reflection, adopted as fundamental principles of action:--

1. That the special object of the Commission was the proper instruction of the freedmen, old and young, in useful and elementary knowledge, religious and secular.

2. That in the establishment of schools it should be done upon consultation with the rector of the parish, where there is one.

3. That the teachers appointed should be of sound principles and approved character.

4. That the providing for the relief of the physical wants of the freedmen, should be subsidiary to the work of education, and that relief should be judiciously distributed by competent agents, consulting with the Clergy when practicable, and in such manner as to avoid, as far as possible the costs of indiscriminate and unnecessary alms-giving.

(Board of Missions, 1866, p. 68)

APPENDIX 4

SCHOOLS AND MISSIONS
1870

The following is a list of the schools and Missions which have been wholly or in part sustained by the Commission:

1. St. Augustine's Normal School at Raleigh, N.C. Principal, the Rev. J. Brinton Smith, D.D. Teachers, 3. Number of pupils, 69-- 36 male, 33 female. Amount appropriated, three thousand dollars; applied as follows: Seventeen hundred and fifty dollars toward the expensed, in board, fuel, and light, of the twenty-five boarding pupils; one hundred and one dollars and seventy-five cents for books, stationery, &c.; and eleven hundred and forty- eight dollars and twenty-five cents towards the support of teachers.

2. High School at Charleston, S.C. Principal, Mrs. Kate B. Savage. Teachers, 6: Miss J. Hammond, Miss E. Johnston, Mrs. E. Ancrum, Miss C. A. Dawson, Samuel Williams; number of scholars, 250; boys, 128; girls, 122. Amount appropriated, two thousand and forty dollars, all of which is paid to the Principal and Teachers.

3. St. Cyprian's School, Newbern, N.C. Teachers 2; Miss M. J. Hicks and Mr. A. Bass. Scholars, 130. Appropriation, $690.

4. St. Augustine's School, .Newbern, N.C. Teachers, 2; Miss S. G. Swetland and M. Williams. Scholars, 100. Appropriation, $690.

5. St. Barnabas' School, Wilmington, N.C. Teachers, 2; Misses. A. Hesketh and E. J. Kennedy. Scholars, 120. Appropriation, $1,100.

6. Mission School, Wilmington, N.C. Teacher, 1; Rev. C. O. Brady. Scholars, 60. Appropriation, $450.

7. Mission School, Fayetteville, N.C. Teachers, 2; Mrs. M. C. Hall and Miss A. C. Hall. Scholars, 91. Appropriation, $720.

8. Mission School, Asheville, N.C. Teacher, 1; Miss A. L. Chapman. Scholars, 46. Appropriation, $85.

9. St. James' School, Norfolk, Va. Teachers, 3; Rev. N. Durant, Miss F. E. Williams, and F. S. Newton. Scholars, 140. Appropriation, $1,138.

10. St. Stephen's School, Petersburg, Va. Teachers, 3; Rev. J. S. Atwell, Mrs. Atwell, and Miss S. L. Brown. Scholars, 120. Appropriation, $435.

11. St. Mark's School, Richmond, Va. Teachers, 2; Mr. and Mrs. Cooley. Scholars, 69. Appropriation, $90.

12. Chapel School, Bolivar, Tenn. Teacher, 1; I. Jones. Scholars, 38. Appropriation, $66.50.

13. St. Cyprian's School, Canfield Orphan Asylum, Memphis, Tenn. Teachers, 2; Mr. J. Lyons and Assistant. Scholars, 40. Appropriation, $350.

14. Mission School, Berne, Camden County, Ga. Teachers, 4; Scholars, 65. No appropriation, the Teachers Mr. and Mrs. Virgil Hilyer and assistants, giving their services gratuitously.

15. Schools in Kentucky under the supervision and control of the Right Rev. Bishop Smith. Teachers, 5. Scholars, 200. Appropriation, $800.

Total Schools, (exclusive of night-schools and some 20 schools open only a portion of the year) 19; Teachers: Clergy, Laymen and Laywomen, 39; Scholars, 2069.

(Board of Missions, 1870, p. 31.)

SCHOOLS AND MISSIONS

1877

The following is a list of the Schools and Missions which are connected with the Commission:

1. St. Augustine's Normal School, Raleigh, N.C. Principal, Rev. J. E. C. Smedes. Assistants, Mr. George A.C. Cooper, Miss Annie Haywood, Miss Jane Thomas. Number of pupils, 120. Boarders, 38.

2.   High School, Charleston, S.C.   Acting Principal, Mrs. E. Ancrum.   Assistants, Miss E. Johnstone, Miss C. A. Dawson, Miss L. W. Peronneau.   Scholars (boys 129, girls 119), 248.

3.   Rev. J. V. Welch, Missionary, Charleston.   Baptisms, 43. Confirmations, 11. Sunday-school, 126. Teachers, 10. Services, 258. Stations, 3. Communicants, 197. Offerings, 345.01.

4.   Edgefield. Rev. E. T. Walker, Rector of Trinity Church and Evangelist.

5.   St. Luke's Church, Columbia, S.C. Rector, Rev. B. Babbit. Mr. T. Saltus, Lay Reader. Confirmations, 19. Communicants, 45. Offerings, $441.59.

6.   St. Barnabas School, Wilmington, N.C. Principal, Miss Alice Brady. Scholars, 158.

7.   St. Mark's Church, Wilmington, N.C. Rev. C. O. Brady. Baptisms, 36. Communicants added, 18. Communicants, 160. Sunday-school, 125; Teachers, 12. Offerings, 792.16.

8.   St. Augustine's School, New Berne, N.C. Principal, Miss S.G. Swetland. Assistant, Mr. A. Bass. Scholars, 200.

9.   St. Cyprian's Chapel, New Berne. Rev. E.M. Forbes. Sunday-school, Teachers, 10; Scholars 118.

10.   St. Joseph's Church and School, Fayetteville, N.C. Rev. A. A. Benton. Teacher, Miss Cain. Scholars, 40. Sunday-school, Teachers, 9; Scholars, 50. Baptisms, 30. Confirmations, 15. Communicants, 72. Offerings, $134.

11.   Mission, Asheville, N.C. Rev. S.V. Berry. Scholars, 101. Sunday-school, 140. Baptisms, 25. Confirmations, 9. Communicants, 29. Offerings, $38.

12.   St. Augustine's Chapel, Raleigh, N.C. Rector, Rev. J.E.C. Smedes. Teacher, Mr. W. R. Harris. Sunday-school, 80. Day Scholars, 80. Baptisms, 4. Confirmations, 5. Communicants, 50. Offerings, $151.

13.   Charlotte, N.C., Rev. W. G. McKinney, Missionary.

14.   Mission School, Elkin, Surrey County, N.C. Sunday-school Scholars, 103.

15.   Washington, D.C. St. Mary's Church, Rev. A. Crummell, D.D. Missions, 3. Communicants, 102. Parish School, 1. Assistant, Rev. A. A. Roberts. Baptisms, 12. Sunday-

schools, 3. Teachers, 20. Scholars, 215. Offerings, $361.69.

16. St. Stephen's Parish and School. Rector, Rev. Gs B. Cooke. Teachers, 8. Scholars, 150. Communicants, 58. Offerings, $66.54.

17. St. Philip's Chapel and School, Richmond. Rector, Rev. J. Peterkin, D.D. Deacon in Charge, Rev. J.R. Winchester. Lay Reader, Wm. N. Gibson. Teachers, J. T. Cooley, Mrs. Cooley. Scholars, 85. Sunday-school, 120. Teachers, 10.

18. McFarland's Station, Lunenburg Co., Va. Principal, Mrs. M. M. Jennings. Assistant, Wm. N. Jennings. Scholars, 95. Sunday-school, 80.

19. Mission School, Clover, Halifax Co., Va. Mrs. Mary E. Miles, James P. De Viney. Scholars, 172.

20. Fairfax Co. Mr. J. R. Johnson, Evangelist, under Rev. Jno. McGill.

21. Mission of Christ Church, Alexandria. Meade Chapel. Rev. W.M. Dame, Rector. Reader and Candidate for Orders, John H.M. Pollard. Scholars, 60. Sunday-school, Teachers, 13; Scholars, 100.

22. St. Stephen's Parish, Savannah, Ga. Rector, Rev. W. H. Morris. Communicants, 158. Baptisms, 20. Confirmations, 27. Sunday-school, 78. Teachers, 8. Offerings, $1,428.62.

23. St. Augustine's Mission and School, Savannah. James Symons, Lay Reader. Communicants, 30.

24. Ogeechee River, St. Mark's Church. Rev. H. Dunlop, Evangelist and Missionary. Geo. Greene, Esq., Postulant, Teacher, and Lay Reader. Baptisms, 17. Confirmations, 7. Communicants, 130. Satilla River, Church of the Messiah.

25. Tenn., Bolivar. St. Philip's Chapel. Rev. W. C. Gray. Baptisms, 3. Communicants, 15. Sunday-school, 40. Offerings, $64.

26. Immanuel Church, Memphis, Tenn. Rector, Rev. G. White, D.D. Deacon, Rev. J. B. McConnell. Communicants, 33. Sunday-school Teacher, 1. Pupils, 9. Offerings, $240.45 27. Rev. G. H. Jackson, Memphis, Missionary.

28. Church of Our Merciful Saviour, Louisville, Ky. Rev. J.T. Helm, Missionary. Baptisms, 47. Confirmations, 13. Communicants, 40. Parish School Teachers, 2. Scholars, 70.

Sunday-school Teachers, 8. Scholars, 90. Sustained wholly by a Presbyter of the Diocese.

29. Hoffman School, Frankfort, Kentucky. Teacher, 1. Scholars, 41.

30. Church of the Good Samaritan, St. Louis, Missouri. Rev. Jas. E. Thompson. Sunday-school, 55. Day-school, Scholars, 55.

31. Fernandina, Fla. Rev. O. P. Thackara. Lay Reader, 1.

32. Key West. St. Peter's Church. Rev. J.H. Young. Confirmations, 12.

33. Jacksonvile, Fla. Under charge of Rev. R. H. Weller.

34. Mobile, Good Shepherd, Ala. Rev. J. A. Massey, D.D.

35. St. Thomas' Mission, New Orleans. C. H. Thompson, D.D., Candidate for Orders. Sam'l M. Wiggins, Lay Reader. Communicants, 20.

36. Pittsburg, Pa. St. Cyprian's Mission. Rev. W.F. Floyd. Sunday-school, 26.

37. Dry Grove, Mississippi. Rev. W.K. Douglas, D.D. Sunday- schools, 3. Scholars, 300. Industrial Schools, 2. Congregations, 2.

Schools and Missions, 37; exclusive of Night Schools and schools open only a portion of the year. Teachers and Missionaries, 55.

(Board of Missions, 1877, pp. 63-64)

APPENDIX 5

Board of Missions, 1870

The present condition of the several Schools is unfolded in the Reports from the several Principals and Teachers presented at the close of the last scholastic year, and herewith submitted, and from which the following extracts are taken. The remaining Reports, in part, have appeared already in THE SPIRIT OF MISSIONS.

ST. AUGUSTINE'S NORMAL SCHOOL, RALEIGH, N.C.—ANNUAL REPORT OF THE PRINCIPAL.

"A committee of the Board of Trustees and many friends of the pupils were present at the closing of the School, to witness the examination, which embraced all the classes. The studies on which they were examined were geography, grammar, arithmetic and natural science; these, with spelling, reading and writing constituting the studies of the past term. There were also exercises in composition and declamation.

The pupils universally acquitted themselves well; as well, in my opinion, as any scholars could have done, whose advantages had been no greater than theirs. The examination in grammar and arithmetic was particularly interesting, it being generally supposed that colored children are not capable of making progress in these studies. Our pupils gave evidence of the exercise of mind and the development of thought. Patience and perseverance will accomplish great results among these people.

During the last term we had eighty applicants, of whom we received sixty-nine, thirty-six males and thirty-three females. We had during the greater part of the term twenty-five boarding pupils from different portions of the State.

Nearly all the boarding pupils during the past term, as well as of the previous terms, are engaged in teaching. We have furnished already at least forty teachers for the colored children of the State. We do not claim that they are fully prepared to teach; by no means; but they are much in advance of those who have not had their training and discipline. We have good reports from our pupils every where.

Several of the pupils were confirmed by Bishop Atkinson, at his last visitation. There were seven of the boarding pupils in the number. These were raised outside of the Protestant Episcopal Church.

There has been with us during the past term a colored man from Connecticut, who is looking forward to the Sacred Ministry. His influence has been most beneficial in every way upon the other pupils. He expects to return and to continue with us until he is ordained.

The boarding pupils have shown, during the past term, a greater disposition to labor, when it has been necessary. We hope they will improve still more in the future, and that they will acquire that self-respect which will prevent them from receiving gratuitous aid in board or instruction.

I am more and more satisfied that our Church is the only means under God for the preservation and elevation of the colored people. We have very little hold upon them at present, owing to the political agitations that are sweeping continually over the South. The politicians are the great agents of influence, and political questions absorb all others in the colored people's minds. The time will come, however, when these agitations will cease and then our Church may expect to be felt.

We are erecting from the funds of the School, with the aid of the additional Bureau, boarding houses for girls and boys, separate, with an building for dining-room and kitchen.

I had an application the other day, from a Clergyman of the Church, for ten colored teachers, which I could not furnish, as all our scholars, that were competent, were already engaged.

Our School is doing a sound, healthful work for the Church and the best interest of the colored people. I hope the Commission may meet with the support from our Clergy and Laity, which it so evidently deserves."

The Commission are gratified to know from the Rt. Rev. Bishop Atkinson, that he has a very favorable opinion of the state and condition of this school and that he esteems its efficient support a matter of prime importance to the great work of the civilization and Christianization to the African race at the South.

HIGH SCHOOL, CHARLESTON, S.C.—ANNUAL REPORT OF THE PRINCIPAL.

"THE School re-opened on the 4th of October, 1869, with six teachers and one hundred and fifty-nine pupils. During that month our number increased to two hundred and thirty-three; and at the present time two hundred and fifty names stand registered on our Book of Entry (boys, one hundred and twenty-eight; girls, one hundred and twenty-two;) ranging in age from five to seventeen years. The average attendance, during the year, has varied from two hundred to two hundred and twenty-three.

We have eight grades in the School, in which are embraced the following studies: Alphabet, Primer—more advanced classes through a series of *five* 'National Readers'.—Geography, both Local and Descriptive, History, Grammar, and Mental and Written Arithmetic. In addition to these secular studies, we have special Religious Instruction on Fridays, by the Clergy of the Local Committee. The elder girls have been formed into a Bible-class, and are instructed by the Rev. Mr. Prentiss. The boys and younger children have been regularly taught by the Rev. C. P. Gadsden, until within the last two months, when ill-health compelled him to absent himself, since which time the Rev. Mr. Prentiss has performed Mr. Gadsden's duties also.

In December last, one of the teachers having withdrawn from the School, one of the elder boys from my class was selected to fill the vacancy temporarily; and although he lacks experience and confidence somewhat, yet he has done very well, and given satisfaction in that position up to this time. Indeed, all the Teachers have worked with hearty zeal, evincing the deepest interest in the moral and intellectual improvement of their pupils. Many of the children who did not know their letters on first entering the school, can now read very well, and have been promoted as their progress allowed. The majority seem anxious to learn, and some of them, I think, possess capacities for the acquisition of knowledge in no way inferior to many who have become not only useful members of society, but distinguished alike for their shining talents and Christian virtues. Altogether we have much to encourage us in the present condition of our Mission School.

The tuition for pupils during the year has amounted to two hundred and twenty-three dollars and five cents ($223.05), which by judicious and economical management has supplied fuel, stationery, and defrayed many other little incidental expenses of the School, during the year, besides enabling us to pay off quite a *large balance* (on a debt of one hundred and twenty-one dollars). A bill of thirty dollars for repairs to the roof of the School-house was also paid, during last winter, from this source. A balance of $9.00 of this tuition money still remains on hand.

In closing this Report, I beg leave in behalf of all the Teachers, to present their united thanks to the Commission for their kind and prompt responses to the demands made upon them for the support of the School."

In addition to the foregoing Report, the following interesting and satisfactory letter, dated Oct. 1, 1870, has been received by the Office Secretary, from the Rev. C. P. Gadsden, of Charleston, S. C.:

LETTER.

"In reply to your inquiry concerning the Franklin Street School for colored children in Charleston, it gives me pleasure to bear testimony, as an eye-witness, of its usefulness. We are much indebted to the Commission for enabling us to provide instruction, under the influence of our Church, for those among whom there is so wide and interesting a field for Missionary labor. When the School was first opened the applications for admission far exceeded our ability to do justice to the pupils, and from time to time we have been compelled to reduce our numbers to the two hundred, whom six teachers can very well attend to. If you could know the interest which the ladies employed by the Commission take in their charge, and mark the regard of the children for their teachers, you would at once perceive that the School has been well conducted. Several of the clergy in the city take a deep personal interest in it, and make it a part of their parochial charge. Every Friday one or more of these

brethren are present, and, in connection with religious exercises, instruct in the Bible, the Church Catechism, and the great truths and duties of Christianity. A special Bible Class for the larger girls, conducted by the Rector of Calvary Church (one of our colored churches), has proved a work of mutual pleasure to both teachers and scholars; and it is hoped may be the means of creating a bond of sympathy between the School and that particular parish. The children welcome the visits of the pastors; and all who have taken part in this instruction regard these children as a portion of the Flock of Christ to whom they are drawn with tender solicitude. You would be much interested in the ready answers of the Creed and children, and could not fail to enjoy their repeating of the Creed and Lord's Prayer, and the hearty and united singing. When the scholars are dismissed, one or more of the clergy remain, and there is a pleasant interchange of opinion with the teachers in regard to the conduct of the School, the incidents of the week, the encouragements of the work, &c. We try to realize that it is work for *Christ* that we are engaged in, and that this School is designed to be a Mission of the Church, in which, while the best intellectual culture is aimed at, the seeking of redeemed souls, to be brought to Jesus and saved through His grace, is never to be lost sight of. We have great cause for thankfulness in the fact that the fine, eligible building, in which the School is gathered, has been secured for this object, and is held by a committee of Churchmen, white and colored, who take a warm interest in the work. To the energy and zeal of the Rev. Mr. Porter we are chiefly indebted for this advantage; and our thanks should be rendered to Gen. Howard for his generous and efficient aid in securing this result. May we not hope now that our School will be a permanent institution, providing for the poor of Christ's family among our colored families a higher culture, and sending forth Christian men and women, and—if it shall please God by His Holy Spirit to call them to the work—pastors, of their own race, to preach the Gospel among the Freedmen of the South? Our Bishop has visited this School, and is grateful for the aid which it has extended to a department of Diocesan work in which he has ever taken the truest interest; and a committee of Clergymen and laymen, elected by the Convention, have cordially coöperated in an effort which we feel to be of the utmost importance for the religious welfare of our colored brethren.

Could the members of our Church throughout this land realize what a wide and inviting Missionary field is opened among the multitudes of our colored fellow-citizens, in city and country; how impressible they are to religious influence; how exposed to unchristian teaching; how accessible to all who have kindness and sympathy for them; how ready to bear the Gospel, and how destitute of the ordinances of Christ: surely they would feel the responsibility, and put forth an effort in their behalf

Our schools should be multiplied, churches should be organized among them, and Missionaries sent in greater numbers, and, when properly qualified, of their own color, to preach the unsearchable riches of CHRIST. The harvest is great, but the laborers few. The South cannot do the work without aid from the North; and can any effort be found better suited to weld our hearts together in the love of JESUS, and in concern for the souls for which He shed His Blood? Our School in Charleston is but a small point on the wide field of labor which spreads around; but seed sown here may bear fruit which shall contribute to the extension of the glorious Gospel of the Blessed SAVIOUR. We beg you not to overlook us,—not to be weary of the work. The ladies who have charge of this School are laboring in love and patience; they work for CHRIST and His Kingdom. Dependent, as each one of them is, upon their daily labor for support, let them not starve in the cause of the MASTER. These little ones whom they teach are dear to JESUS, and should be the wards of His Church. I would most earnestly commend this School to the prayers and liberality of members of our Church."

ST. AUGUSTINE'S SCHOOL, NEWBERNE, N, C.—FROM THE REPORT OF MISS SWETLAND.

"I HAVE now been nearly four years in this field, and during that time the general aspect of things has greatly changed, and I find it difficult to separate results so as to be able to determine which definitely belong to ourselves. In the first place, the colored people are really at work, fairly earning a subsistence for themselves, and their physical condition is greatly improved. The increased demand for laborers has been followed by quite a stampede to the country, and among those that remain is manifested a most praiseworthy anxiety for employment. Even children seek opportunities to earn a trifle towards their support—selling berries, tending cows, watching cornfields, etc., and they certainly deserve credit for their efforts. Of course this necessity for toil affects our Schools so far as punctual attendance is concerned, and another year will more fully sift the matter and bring to us, or rather, leave us with those from whom we can expect more specific fruits to the Church. A slight decrease in numbers could not be considered a misfortune.

"My greatest number of scholars at any one time during the present term has been one hundred and thirty, and of these, I think not more than forty were my pupils last year. Many of the old scholars are scattered abroad through the State, yet, the instruction once given is not lost; they have gone with their Testaments and Prayer-Books, and also with the ability to read them. Let us hope the seed may spring up in waste places.

"I have before mentioned to you that St. Augustine's is in the outskirts of the town, in the midst of a dusky population, and these people, at least all who profess any religion, are Baptists and Methodists. I have not one

child from a Church family, hence the Catechism and Prayer-Book seem of no importance to them; indeed, it is literally 'compelling them to come in;' but is there not an implied promise in Scripture for such as these? Of those mentioned, only one was found without the 'wedding garment!' During some months the Morning Service was daily conducted by Mr. Weston, and for this favor we owe many thanks to Mr. Forbes and Mr. W., but of late Mr. Weston's duties have called him elsewhere, and the prayers and Psalter have again been read by myself. Our children are familiar with the entire Service and are well versed in the Catechism. Their advancement in Reading, Writing, Arithmetic and Geography is very fair; their acquaintance with the Maps is decidedly good. Whilst failing to perceive any great general results from our efforts, I can still point to instances of marked advantage in individual cases. Do you recollect my once alluding to an Isaac Smith, a hopeful scholar of last year who went off in vacation to the country and taught where before there had been no one to instruct at all? He returned to me in October, but there was so much raw material on hand, I had not time to give him the attention I thought he required; so Mr. Forbes procured his admission to the Normal School at Raleigh, and we have recently been baptized and confirmed. His brother Charles is my pupil this year, and he, too, is faithful and studious, a Sunday-School Teacher, correct and serious in deportment. He bids fair to become a useful man and an honor to his race. In truth, I might cite a number of cases that tell of a little something accomplished; and I reproach myself that I ever feel discouraged; but an eye that looks upon but one thing is likely to be influenced by every passing phase of that one object."

ST. BARNABAS' SCHOOL, WILMINGTON, N. C.—FROM THE REPORT OF MISS HESKETH.

"OUR School has closed after a pleasant and encouraging session of nearly nine months. I say encouraging, because our scholars have done so well. They have attended regularly at all times, and improved in their studies. Each new month we have had nearly one hundred and thirty names enrolled, with a daily attendance of one hundred and twenty, until the 1st of May, when several left to work on farms.

We have been teaching in our schools, reading, spelling, writing and arithmetic to all, with two or three classes composed of twenty-five or thirty pupils in Geography. Also the Church Catechism to all, with different parts of the Church Services.

These lessons have been recited and explained every day, and the greater part of the children have evinced much interest in them and improved greatly.

As far as we have taken them in these studies, they understand a

readily as any children. Much to our regret, many of our larger boys and girls are obliged to leave school so soon. They get along nicely, and then situations are procured for them. Their parents are poor and with large families, and they must necessarily leave school and go to procure bread and clothing. We find, too, that they who are anxious to learn and become intelligent men and women, are also ready to work, and, of course, preferred to those who are less ambitious.

The parents, too, in a great measure, are industrious, hard-working people. Hard-working for them here ; for we have come to the conclusion that one cannot work as they would in the North, or in a colder climate.

It is painful to see how idle and improvident some of these people are. Yet, on second thought, we are expecting too much from them. For where is there a city, town, or village, in which we cannot find these evils indulged in, and, by people supposed to be far superior to these in good judgment and common sense?

We may not have come in contact with the most miserable of these people, but, as far as we can see, and with an impartial view to all, they are doing admirably. Two years ago, in the neighborhood of our school-house, there was scarcely a house to be seen on the north and east side of us. Now, close to the building, and on all sides, houses are closely built and inhabited. A lot of ground has been purchased at first, and then a frame put up, and with laths only, and with windows, as also doors boarded, they have been occupied. Fires are made outside until money can be obtained for building chimneys, and so, little by little is done until the building is completed, to the great joy of the occupants. Some of these little houses are very pretty and neat. Surely then, some one of the family has worked hard, starting to build as they do with nothing but the weekly wages they may receive.

The time and money we have expended here have not been wasted, I can assure you."

MISSION SCHOOL, FAYETTEVILLE, N. C.—FROM THE REPORT OF MRS. HALL.

"IT is somewhat difficult to make an exact return of our School; sometimes pupils begin in the middle of the month, attend two or three weeks, and then, having an offer of employment, leave, and being absent perhaps two or three weeks or more, return. It is hard to know how to count them, and I sometimes in my reports omit them altogether, though they are some of my favorite pupils and, although irregular, manage to learn a great deal. Sometimes they only come one hour, or perhaps at recess, recite their lessons and return to their home duties. These are generally grown women who are anxious to learn. A few come to my house after dinner, and others again, generally grown, come after candle-

light. All these I have never mentioned in my reports, their attendance is not always regular and varies from six to ten in number. This part of my teaching is very interesting to me. I look on it as purely Missionary work. It gives me great pleasure to know that hard-working men have commenced with Primers and left, being able to read their Bibles. Of these outside pupils, three were confirmed at Bishop Atkinson's last visitation. One of my favorite girls, who has been very a regular attendant of the School about two years and has been very exemplary in all things, about a month ago took charge of one of the district schools. She commenced with a Primer. She is a young married woman, and became a Communicant last year. I mention her with pride.

Our School will compare well with the white Benevolent School-children, who have about the same home advantages. The parents of my scholars are uniformly kind and respectful to me, and always enforce my authority."

CHARACTER OF THE SCHOOLS.

It will not be forgotten that all our Schools are Christian Schools, in which the pupils are educated morally as well as intellectually, and taught the principles of the Gospel of Christ as set forth in the Holy Scripture, and as this Church has received the same. In every case they are under the supervision of the Bishop and Parochial Clergy within whose Jurisdiction they have been planted. More than this, in several cases already, and this is the anticipated result generally, the School has become the nucleus of a Congregation, with its own Pastor of African descent, and with all the varied blessings which grow from such a relation. Thus we have in Norfolk, Petersburgh and Wilmington, established congregations, with the Rev. Messrs. Durant, Atwell and Brady (colored men) as their Ministers.

OUR MISSIONARIES AND TEACHERS.

And here it may be well to put on record the high estimate in which this Commission holds the Missionaries and Teachers in their employ, for ability, fidelity, perseverance and Christian character. A number of these have now served the Church in this department of her work for several years, amid trials, discouragements, and difficulties not a few; and with singular zeal and steadfastness. They deserve the thanks of the Board of Missions,—and especially those Christian ladies who, leaving home and kindred, have sojourned among the objects of the Church's care, solely to do them good: as undoubtedly they have received the benediction of Him Whose example they follow, and Whose Cross they bear.

THE PENNSYLVANIA BRANCH.

The Pennsylvania Branch, after four years of efficient service as our auxiliary, has deemed it expedient, much to our regret, to discontinue its

APPENDIX 6

RESOLUTIONS.

The following Statement, with the subjoined Resolutions, is respectfully commended to the consideration of the Board of Missions.

Whereas, Much has been said and written upon the subject of abolishing the Commission of Home Missions to Colored People, and remanding the work to the Domestic Committee; the members of the Commission deem it due to the Board of Missions, and but just to themselves, to call attention to the following facts.

1. When, twelve years ago, the Mission work among the Colored People was committed to this Commission, it was surrounded and embarrassed by the difficulties and obstacles which could only be removed and overcome by long and patient labor.

2. Notwithstanding these difficulties, and the small amount of means placed at the disposal of the Commission, many evidences of usefulness and success have manifested themselves.

3. At this time, many new fields for the labors of the Commission are presenting themselves, and many and urgent are the requests that they should be occupied.

4. The finances of the Commission have been managed with rigid economy; and now at the close of the Twelfth year, its pecuniary obligations are all discharged and there is a balance in the Treasury of One Thousand Dollars. Therefore,

Resolved, That the members of the Commission think it would be unwise to make any radical changes in the administration of this work,--unless somethin more practical, and promising much greater success, can be substituted in its stead.

Resolved, That it is all important, that the policy of the Church, with regard to this part of her Missionary work, should become settled and permanent,--otherwise, it will be impossible to enlist the sympathies and offerings of our people in its behalf.

October, 1877

(Board of Missions, 1877, p. 84.)

APPENDIX 7

Sub Committee for Work Among Freedmen

1 January 1878

Rev. Chas. H. Hall. D.D. Chairman

Rev. Geo. Leeds D.D.
Rev. W. N. McVickar D. D.
Lemmel Coffin Esqr.
W. G. Lowe Esqr.

Rev. N. H. Schenck D.D.
William Scott Esqr.
Cornelius Vanderbilt Esqr.

Treasurer. Lloyd W. Wells. Esqr.

Secretary. W. E. Webb

(Freedman's Aid Commission, Executive Committee Minutes Book,
 1865-1878, Archives of the Episcopal Church, RG 41-55)

APPENDIX 8

Original Membership of the Commission for Work among Colored
People - 20 December 1886

The Rt. Rev. Dr. Dudley,   The Rev. Dr. A. T. Porter
The Rt. Rev. Dr. H. C. Potter,   The Rev. J. B. Newton
The Rt. Rev. Dr. Randolph,   The Rev. G. B. Cooke
The Rt. Rev. Dr. Paret,   Mr. J. C. Bancroft Davis
The Rt. Rev. Dr. Weed,   Mr. Joseph Bryan
The Rev. Dr. J. H. Eccleston,   Mr J. Pierpoint Morgan*
The Rev. C. B. Perry,   Gen. Kirby Smith   .
              Mr. John W. Atkinson

*Mr J. Pierpoint Morgan declined to serve, and Mr. John A.
King was appointed in his place.

(Board of Missions, 1887, p. 128)

APPENDIX 9

General Appeal Letter
1893

Will you not read, will you not pray for, will you not pray
for, will you not help this cause as speedily and strongly as
you can? As general agent for our Colored work I feel forced
to address this card to some of the earnest-hearted
communicants of our Church. This financial distress upon us
jeopardizes our work. We need $20,000 to hold what we have
gained. Many of our former helpers need help themselves in
these hard times. But God's work must go on even if it
carries to the Cross His loyal ones. Our Church must do her
part to give these 7,470,000 Colored people in the land the
Gospel. Now we have 137 mission stations served by 60 white
and 47 Colored ministers. We have 6,399 communicants, 95
church buildings, 52 schools, 4 hospitals, 1 Church home, 125
Sunday-schools with 4,734 pupils, 3 normal and divinity-
schools with 160 normal and 31 divinity students. The Colored
people paid $22,509 towards these objects. We cannot, we must
not, suffer this work to go back for the want of money. It is
sacred trust from God to every member of His Church.
Christianity alone can save these struggling people. Well we
not arise in loving greatness and strive to give it to them?
The reproach of contracting the work so long as we have the
means, even through severe self-denial to advance it, is what
the the Church dare not permit, for her honor and her loyalty
forbid. I appeal therefore to every brother clergyman to do
something no to tide us over, and then to place this cause
among those regularly presented and helped yearly in his
church. I appeal to every communicant entrusted with means,
by the compassion of Him 'who for our sakes became poor,' to
give as largely and promptly as possible. I appeal to the
poor in purse, but rich in grace, to send at once some help,
be it ever so small and follow it with your prayers. The
crisis is sharp, the need urgent. Help, and help now, as God
gives you power. Send all offerings to Mr. George Bliss,
Treasurer, 22 Bible House, New York, marked 'Colored Work.'

Your fellow-worker for Christ and His Church,
C. C. Penick, General Agent for the Commission,
Charlestown, West Virginia.

(Spirit of Missions, 1893, p. 299.)

ENDNOTES

Chapter 1

[1] John F. W. Ware, <u>The Danger of Today</u> (Sermon preached at the First Independent Church; Baltimore, Md.: Chushings & Bailey, 1865), pp. 14-15.

[2] Winthrop D. Jordan, <u>White Over Black: American Attitudes Toward the Negro, 1550-1812</u> (New York: W.W. Norton & Company, 1977), p. 44.

[3] Jordan, p. 56.

[4] Nathaniel S. Wheaton, <u>A Discourse on St. Paul's Epistle to Philemon Exhibiting the Duty of Citizens of the Northern States in regard to the Institution of Slavery</u> (Hartford, Conn.: Tiffany & Co., 1851), pp. 22-23.

[5] Anthony Schuyler, <u>Slaveholding as a Religious Question</u> (Sermon preached in Christ Church, Oswego: 1861), p. 9.

[6] John H. Hopkins, <u>A Scriptural, Ecclesiastical & Historical View of Slavery from the Day of the Patriarch Abraham, to the Nineteenth Century</u> (New York: W.I. Pooley & Co., 1864), p. 15.

[7] Leon F. Litwack, <u>Been in the Storm So Long: The Aftermath of Slavery</u> (New York: Vintage Books, 1980), p. 68.

[8] Litwack, p. 71.

[9] Litwack, p. 80.

[10] Litwack, p. 81.

[11] Litwack, pp. 90-91.

[12] Litwack, p. 87.

[13] John M. Blum, ed., <u>The National Experience, Part I--A History of the United States to 1877</u> (New York: Harcourt Brace Jovanovich, 1983), pp. 385.

[14] Litwack, p. 218.

[15] Litwack, p. 280.

[16] Blum, pp. 392-393.

[17] U.S., Congress, House, <u>Report of [Major General]</u> <u>Carl Schurz on the States of South Carolina, Georgia, Alabama,</u> <u>Mississippi, and Louisiana,</u> 39th Cong., 1st sess., 1865, pp. 21 & 35.

[18] Litwack, p. 265.

[19] Litwack, p. 223, as quoted in Miller, Elinor, & Eugene Genovese, eds., <u>Plantation, Town, and County</u> (Urbana, Ill., 1974), p. 360.

Chapter 2

[1] Episcopal Church, <u>Journal of the Proceedings</u> <u>of the Bishops, Clergy, & Laity of the Protestant Episcopal Church</u> <u>in the United States Assembled in General Convention, 1865</u> (Boston: William A. Hall, 1865), p. 305.

[2] General Convention Journal, 1865, p. 175.

[3] See Appendix 1 for the bylaws of the Executive Committee of the Home Missions Commission.

[4] Episcopal Church, Domestic & Foreign Missionary Society, <u>Board of Missions/Managers Annual Meetings, 1866-1878</u> (New York: Various Publishers), pp. 63-64. See Appendix 2 for original membership list of the Home Missions Commission.

[5] General Convention Journal, 1865, p. 175.

[6] Board of Missions, 1866, pp. 68-69. See Appendix 3 for Home Missions Commission's objectives.

[7] <u>Spirit of Missions</u>, Board of Missions of the Protestant Episcopal Church in the U.S.A., vol. 31 (New York: Various Publishers, 1866), p. 220.

[8] Board of Missions, 1866, pp. 64, 68-69.

[9] <u>Spirit of Missions</u>, vol. 31, 1866, p. 93 & Board of Missions, 1866, pp. 66-67.

[10] Board of Missions, 1866, p. 66.

[11] <u>Spirit of Missions</u>, vol. 31, 1866, p. 42.

[12] <u>Spirit of Missions</u>, vol. 31, 1866, pp. 43-44.

[13] Board of Missions, 1866, p. 68.

[14] Board of Missions, 1866, p. 67.

[15] Board of Missions, 1866, p. 68.

[16] Robert A. Bennett, "Black Episcopalians: A History from the Colonial Period to the Present," <u>Historical Magazine of the Protestant Episcopal Church</u>, vol. 43 (1974): 233.

[17] <u>Spirit of Missions</u>, vol. 31, 1866, p. 413.

[18] Board of Missions, 1866, p. 72.

[19] Board of Missions, 1870, p. 39.

[20] All funds were required to be used to further missionary work and could not be used to build school houses or churches. This restriction was not lifted until 1903 when the Dosestic & Foreign Missionary Society gave the Commission persmission to use funds "for the erection, repair, and otherwise securing of proper places of worship." Minutes of the Commission for Work Among Colored People, 21 April 1903, Beverly D. Tucker Mss., Archives of the Episcopal Church, RG 52-76.

[21] Board of Missions, 1867, pp. 43-44 and Board of Missions, 1877, pp. 62-64; Also see Appendix 4 for a listing of schools.

[22] Board of Missions, 1877, pp. 60-61.

[23] Board of Missions, 1878, p. 446.

[24] Board of Missions, 1867, p. 44.

[25] Board of Missions, 1875, p. 57.

[26] See Appendix 5 for various reports of missionaries.

[27] Freedman's Aid Commission, Executive Minutes, 27 June 1867, p. 71, Archives of the Episcopal Church, RG 41-55.

[28] Board of Missions, 1877, p. 65 & <u>Spirit of Missions</u>, vol. 42, 1877, pp. 39-40.

[29] Board of Missions, 1877, p. 65.

[30] Spirit of Missions, vol. 42, 1877, pp. 599-600.

[31] Board of Missions, 1875, p. 51.

[32] Board of Missions, 1876, pp. 64-67.

[33] Board of Missions, 1876, p. 66.

[34] Board of Missions, 1866, pp. 69-70.

[35] Board of Missions, 1868, pp. 66-67.

[36] H. Peers Brewer, "The Protestant Episcopal Freedman's Commission, 1865-1878," Historical Magazine of the Protestant Episcopal Church, vol. 26 (March 1957): pp. 377-378.

[37] Winthrop D. Jordan, White Over Black (New York: N.N. Norton & Co., 1977), pp. 90-91.

[38] H. Peers Brewer, pp. 377-378.

[39] Board of Missions, 1873, p. 46.

[40] Spirit of Missions, vol. 31, 1866, pp. 95-96.

[41] Spirit of Missions, vol. 31, 1866, p. 219.

[42] Spirit of Missions, vol. 31, 1866, p. 219.

[43] Spirit of Missions, vol. 31, 1866, p. 219.

[44] Spirit of Missions, vol 31, 1866, p. 219.

[45] Board of Missions, 1870, p. XX.

[46] Spirit of Missions, vol. 42, 1877, p. 458 & H. Peers Brewer, p. 379.

[47] Spirit of Missions, vol. 42, 1877, pp. 516-518 & H. Peers Brewer, p. 379.

[48] Spirit of Missions, vol. 42, 1877, p. 619. See Appendix 6 for Home Missions' resolution against dissolving the Commission.

[49] Board of Missions, 1886, p. 6.

[50] Board of Missions, 1874, p. 70.

[51] Board of Missions, 1875, p. 55.

[52] Spirit of Missions, vol. 31, 1866, pp. 287-288.

[53] Spirit of Missions, vol. 32, 1867, p. 77.

[54] Spirit of Missions, vol. 32, 1867, p. 77.

[55] Spirit of Missions, vol. 32, 1867, p. 249.

[56] Spirit of Missions, vol. 32, 1867, p. 77.

[57] Spirit of Missions, vol. 32, 1867, p. 78.

[58] Spirit of Missions, vol. 32, 1867, p. 78.

[59] Spirit of Missions, vol. 32, 1867, p. 87.

[60] Spirit of Missions, vol. 32, 1867, p. 249.

[61] Spirit of Missions, vol. 32, 1867, p. 251.

[62] Spirit of Missions, vol. 32, 1867, p. 549.

[63] Spirit of Missions, vol. 32, 1867, p. 549.

[64] Board of Missions, 1869, p. 64.

[65] Board of Missions, 1869, p. 64.

[66] Board of Missions, 1870, p. 39.

[67] Freedman's Aid Commission, Executive Minutes, 1 January 1878, notation, Archives of the Episcopal Church, RG 41-55. See Appendix 7 for Subcommittee for Work Among Freedmen formed in Domestic Missions Department after the cessation of the Home Missions Commission.

[68] Board of Missions, 1871, p. 77.

Chapter 3

[1] Episcopal Church, Diocese of Maryland, Journal of the Eighty-Fourth Annual Convention of the Protestant Episcopal Church in Maryland, 1867 (Printed by Convention, 1867), p. 103.

[2] Diocese of Maryland, 1867, p. 103.

[3] Diocese of Maryland, 1867, p. 103.

[4] Diocese of Maryland, 1867, p. 103.

[5] Episcopal Church, Diocese of Virginia, Journal of the Seventy-Second Annual Council of the Protestant Episcopal Church in Virginia, 1867 (Richmond, Va.: Medical Journal Printers, 1867), p. 57.

[6] Diocese of Virginia, 1867, pp. 58-59.

[7] Diocese of Virginia, 1867, p. 59.

[8] Diocese of Virginia, 1867, p. 58.

[9] Diocese of Virginia, 1867, p. 58.

[10] Episcopal Church, Diocese of Virginia, Journal of the Seventy-Third Annual Council in the Protestant Episcopal Church in Virginia, 1868 (Richmond, Va.: Pub. Office of "Farmer's Gazette," 1868), p. 41.

[11] Diocese of Virginia, 1868, pp. 41-42.

[12] Episcopal Church, Diocese of Virginia, Journal of the Seventy-Fourth Annual Council of the Protestant Episcopal Church in Virginia, 1869 (Richmond, Va.: Gary, Clemmitt, & Jones, 1869), p. 56.

[13] Episcopal Church, Diocese of Virginia, Journal of the Seventy-Sixth Annual Council of the Protestant Episcopal Church in Virginia, 1871 (Richmond, Va.: Clemmitt & Jones, 1871), p. 51.

[14] Episcopal Church, Diocese of Georgia, Journal of the Fifty-First Annual Convention of the Protestant Episcopal Church in the Diocese of Georgia, 1873 (Savannah, Ga.: Morning News Steam-Power Press, 1873), p. 26.

[15] Diocese of Georgia, 1873, p. 26.

[16] Episcopal Church, Diocese of Georgia, Journal of the Fifty-Fourth Annual Convention of the Protestant Episcopal Church in the Diocese of Georgia, 1876 (Augusta, Ga.: Chronicle & Sentinel, 1876), p. 78.

[17] Episcopal Church, Diocese of Tennessee, Journal of the Thirty-Eighth Annual Convention of the Protestant Episcopal Church in the Diocese of Tennessee, 1870 (Memphis,

Tenn.: Southwestern Pub. Co., 1870), p. 29

[18] Episcopal Church, Diocese of Tennessee, Journal of the Proceedings of the Thirty-Fourth Annual Convention of the Protestant Episcopal Church in the Diocese of Tennessee, 1866 (Memphis, Tenn.: Hutton, Brower & Co., 1866), p. 58 & Diocese of Tennessee, 1870, p. 28.

[19] Episcopal Church, Diocese of Tennessee, Journal of the Proceedings of the Thirty-fifth Annual Convention of the Protestant Episcopal Church in the Diocese of Tennessee, 1867 (Memphis, Tenn.: C.F. Chamberlin & Co, 1867), p. XXVIII.

[20] Diocese of Tennessee, 1867, p. XXVIII.

[21] Diocese of Tennessee, 1867, pp. XXVIII & XXIX.

[22] Diocese of Tennessee, 1867, p. 40.

[23] Episcopal Church, Diocese of Tennessee, Journal of the Thirty-Seventh Annual Convention of the Protestant Episcopal Church in the Diocese of Tennessee, 1869 (Memphis, Tenn.: Southwestern Publishing Co., 1869), p. 28.

[24] Diocese of Tennessee, 1869, p. 26.

[25] Diocese of Tennessee, 1869, p. 26.

[26] Episcopal Church, Diocese of Tennessee, Journal of the Proceedings of the Sixtieth Annual Convention of the Protestant Episcopal Church in the Diocese of Tennessee, 1892 (Sewanee, Tenn.: Universtiy of the South Press, 1892), p. 48.

[27] Episcopal Church, Diocese of Tennessee, Journal of the Proceedings of the Forty-Second Annual Convention of the Protestant Episcopal Church in the Diocese of Tennessee, 1874 (Memphis, Tenn.: Boyle & Chapman, 1874), p. 60.

[28] Diocese of Tennessee, 1874, p. 60.

[29] Episcopal Church, Diocese of Tennessee, Journal of the Proceedings of the Forty-Third Annual Convention of the Protestant Episcopal Church in the Diocese of Tennessee, 1875 (Memphis, Tenn.: Boyle & Chapman, 1875), p. ?

[30] Episcopal Church, Diocese of North Carolina, Journal of the Fiftieth Annual Convention of the Protestant Episcopal Church in the State of North Carolina , 1866 (Fayetteville, N.C., 1866), p. 18.

[31] Diocese of North Carolina, 1866, p. 18.

[32] Episcopal Church, Diocese of North Carolina, Journal of the Fifty-First Annual Convention of the Protestant Episcopal Church in the State of North Carolina, 1867 (Fayetteville, N.C., 1867), p. 48.

[33] Episcopal Church, Diocese of North Carolina, Journal of the Fifty-Second Annual Convention of the Protestant Episcopal Church in the State of North Carolina, 1868 (Wilmington, N.C.: Wm. H. Bernard's Pub. House, 1868), p. 31.

[34] Episcopal Church, Diocese of North Carolina, Journal of the Fifty-Seventh Annual Convention of the Protestant Episcopal Church in the State of North Carolina, 1873, (Raleigh, N.C.: Edwards, Broughton & Co., 1873), pp. 98-100; Diocese of North Carolina, Journal of the Sixty-First Annual Convention, 1877, pp. 210-212; Diocese of North Carolina, 1868, pp. 126-128.

[35] Diocese of North Carolina, 1867, p. 26.

[36] Episcopal Church, Diocese of North Carolina, Journal of the Fifty-Ninth Annual Convention of the Protestant Episcopal Church in the Diocese of North Carolina, 1875 (Goldsboro, N.C.: Messenger & J.B. Whitaker, Jr., 1875), p. 53.

[37] Diocese of North Carolina, 1875, p. 53.

Chapter 4

[1] Episcopal Church, Domestic & Foreign Missionary Society. Board of Managers Annual Meeting, 1879, p. 407.

[2] Board of Managers, 1879, pp. 407-408.

[3] Spirit of Missions, Board of Missions of the Protestant Episcopal Church in the U.S.A., vol. 43 (New York: Various Publishers, 1878), p. 47.

[4] Letter to the editor of the Churchman from C. C. Penick, 5 March 1894, St. Mark's Library of The General Theological Seminary, Howard Chandler Robbins Collection, Item No. 117.

[5] Spirit of Missions, vol. 43, 1878, p. 111.

[6] Spirit of Missions, vol. 48, 1883, p. 125.

[7] Spirit of Missions, vol. 43, 1878, p. 111.

[8] Spirit of Missions, vol. 51, 1886, p. 360.

[9] Spirit of Missions, vol. 43, 1878, pp. 48-49.

[10] Spirit of Missions, vol. 50, 1885, pp. 250-252.

[11] Spirit of Missions, vol. 51, 1886, p. 323.

[12] Spirit of Missions, vol. 48, 1883, pp. 219-220.

[13] Board of Managers, 1886, p. 23.

[14] Board of Managers, 1887, p. 128.

[15] Spirit of Missions, vol. 62, p. 223 & Episcopal Church, Journal of the Proceedings of the Bishops, Clergy, & Laity of the Protestant Episcopal Church in the United States of America Assembled in General Convention, 1886 (Printed for the Convention, 1887), p. 182.

[16] Board of Managers, 1887, pp. 15-16 & The General Convention of 1886, p. 224.

[17] Board of Managers, 1887, p. 33.

[18] Board of Managers, 1887, p. 127. See Appendix 8 for listing of original members of the Commission.

[19] Board of Managers, 1887, p. 127.

[20] Board of Managers, 1892, pp. 114-115.

[21] Board of Managers, 1889, pp. 13-14.

[22] Board of Managers, 1889, p. 13-14.

[23] Spirit of Missions, vol. 62, 1897, p. 244 & Board of Managers, 1891, p. 100.

[24] Spirit of Missions, vol. 59, 1894, p. 565.

[25] Spirit of Missions, vol. 62, 1897, pp. 242-243.

[26] Earl Johnson, "Crummell and Onderdonk: The Early Admission Policy of the General Theological Seminary Towards Blacks" (Unpublished Essay, 1977), p. 4.

[27] Spirit of Missions, vol. 49, 1884, p. 175.

[28] Spirit of Missions, vol. 62, 1897, p. 232-233.

[29] Spirit of Missions, vol. 62, 1897, p. 236.

[30] Spirit of Missions, vol. 62, 1897, p. 231.

[31] Spirit of Missions, vol. 62, 1897, p. 231.

[32] Spirit of Missions, vol. 61, 1896, p. 188.

[33] Spirit of Missions, vol. 68, 1903, p. 274.

[34] Spirit of Missions, vol. 67, 1902, pp. 890-891.

[35] Spirit of Missions, vol. 67, 1902, pp. 890-891.

[36] Board of Managers, 1903, p. 185.

[37] Spirit of Missions, vol. 68, 1903, p. 595.

[38] Spirit of Missions, vol. 49, 1884, p. 175.

[39] Spirit of Missions, vol. 67, 1902, p. 419.

[40] Spirit of Missions, vol. 67, 1902, p. 419.

[41] Spirit of Missions, vol. 55, 1890, p. 15.

[42] Spirit of Missions, vol. 55, 1890, p. 15.

[43] Spirit of Missions, vol. 54, 1889, p. 69.

[44] General Convention of 1886, p. 224.

[45] General Convention of 1886, p. 224.

[46] Proceedings of the Board of Managers, Vol. VI, 14 Sept. 1887 to 13 June 1888, Meeting of 13 June 1888, Archives of the Episcopal Church, RG 41-64.

[47] Proceedings of the Board of Managers, Vol. VII, 12 Sept. 1888 to 11 June 1889, Meeting of 11 June 1889, Archives of the Episcopal Church, RG 41-65.

[48] Board of Managers, 1896, pp. 26 & 111 & Board of Managers, 1898, p. 24.

[49] Spirit of Missions, vol. 58, 1893, p. 299. See Apendix 9 for typical appeal letter.

[50] Board of Managers, 1893, p. 97. Bishop Charles

Clifton Penick was consecrated Bishop (117) on 13 February 1877 at St. Paul's Church in Alexandria, Virginia. He became the third bishop of Cape Palmas in West Africa and resigned this post in 1883; he remained a bishop. He then served as rector in various parishes. "Bishops of the Episcopal Church, 1-150, 14 Nov. 1784 - 25 April 1889," General Theological Seminary, St. Mark's Library, Mss.

[52] Spirit of Missions, vol. 61, 1896, p. 318.

[53] Spirit of Missions, vol. 61, 1896, pp. 578-579.

[54] Board of Managers, 1896, p. 16.

[55] Board of Managers, 1896, p. 16.

[56] Board of Managers, 1896, p. 16.

[57] Letter to Bishop Greer from Bishop Satterlee, 12 Dec. 1904, pp. 4 & 5, Henry Satterlee Mss., Archives of the Episcopal Church, RG 52-69.

[58] Board of Managers, 1896, p. 114.

[59] Letter to Langford from Pellew, 31 Oct. 1895, Henry Pellew Mss., Archives of the Episcopal Church, RG 52-63.

[60] Letter to Langford from Pellew, 31 Oct. 1895.

[61] Letter to Langford from Pellew, 31 Oct. 1895.

[62] Spirit of Missions, vol. 61, 1896, p. 221.

[63] Episcopal Church, Proceedings of the Protestant Episcopal Church in the United States of America Assembled in General Convention, 1889 (Printed for Convention, 1890), pp. 50, 51, 77, & 113.

[64] Spirit of Missions, vol. 59, 1892, pp. 216-217.

[65] Board of Managers, 1891, p. 10.

[66] Julia C. Emery. A Century of Endeavor, 1821 - 1921 (New York: Department of Missions, 1921), p. 85.

[67] General Convention of 1889, p. 309.

[68] General Convention of 1889, pp. 337-338.

[69] General Convention of 1889, p. 266.

[70] General Convention of 1889, p. 57.

[71] Letter to Langford from Bishop Paret, 18 Jan. 1892, Paret Mss., Archives of the Episcopal Church, RG 52-61.

[72] Letter to Bishop Greer from Bishop Satterlee, 12 Dec. 1904, Henry Satterlee Mss., Archives of the Episcopal Church, RG 52-69.

[73] Letter to Bishop Greer from Bishop Satterlee, 12 Dec. 1904.

[74] Letter to Bishop Greer from Bishop Satterlee, 12 Dec. 1904.

[75] Minutes of the Commission for Work among Colored People, Meeting of 21 October 1902, Beverly Tucker Mss., Archives of the Episcopal Church, RG 52-76.

[76] Letter to Bishop Greer from Bishop Satterlee, 12 Dec. 1904.

[77] Letter to Bishop Greer from Bishop Satterlee, 12 Dec. 1904.

[78] Board of Managers, 1905, pp. 4-5.

[79] Spirit of Missions, vol. 54, 1898, p. 115.

Chapter 5

[1] See p. 16

[2] See pp. 68, 69, & 99.

[3] See p. 66 & 67.

[4] See p. 20.

[5] See p. 87.

[6] See pp. 62 & 63.

[7] See pp. 45 & 65.

[8] See pp. 22, 26-28, & p. 39.

[9] See pp. 22, 23, & 32.

[10] Letter to Beverly Tucker from John M. Pollard, 10 Agugust 1904, Tucker Mss., Archives of the Episcopal Church, RG 52-76.

[11] See p. 78.

[12] See pp. 84 & 85.

[13] See pp. 37 & 38.

[14] See pp. 81 & 82.

[15] I Corinthians 13:12-13 (Common Bible, Revised Standard Version).

BIBLIOGRAPHY

Addison, James T. The Episcopal Church in the United States, 1789 - 1931. New York: Charles Scribner's Sons, 1951.

Archives of the Episcopal Church. Freedman's Aid Committee Mss.

Archives of the Episcopal Church. S. Lucy Joyner Mss.

Archives of the Episcopal Church. Joint Committee Meetings of the Domestic and Foreign Missionary Society and the Freedman's Aid Committee Mss.

Archives of the Episcopal Church. Paret Mss.

Archives of the Episcopal Church. Pellew Mss.

Archives of the Episcopal Church. Penick Mss.

Archives of the Episcopal Church. Satterlee Mss.

Archives of the Episcopal Church. Tucker Mss.

Archives of the Episcopal Church. Proceedings of the Board of Managers, vols. v, vi, vii, xxii, & xxiii Mss.

Bennett, Robert A. "Black Episcopalians: A History from the Colonial Period to the Present." Historical Magazine of the Protestant Episcopal Church, vol. 43 (1974): 231-245.

The Bible. Revised Standard Version, The Common Bible.

Blum, John M., ed. The National Experience, Part I--A History of the United States to 1877. New York: Harcourt Brace Jovanovich, 1983.

Bragg, George F. Jr. "The Episcopal Church and the Negro Race." Historical Magazine of the Protestant Episcopal Church, vol. 4 (March 1935): 47-52.

Bragg, George F. Jr. History of the Afro-American Group of the Episcopal Church, reprint. New York: Johnson Reprint Corp., 1968.

Brewer, H. Peers. "The Protestant Episcopal Freedman's Commission, 1865-1878." Historical Magazine of the Protestant Episcopal Church, vol. 26 (December 1957):

361-381.

Episcopal Church. Domestic and Foreign Missionary Society.
    Board of Missions of the Protestant Episcopal Church,
    Thirty-First through Forty-Third Annual Meetings, 1865 -
    1877. New York: Various Pub., 1865-1877.

Episcopal Church. Domestic and Foreign Missionary Society.
    Board of Managers of the Domestic and Foreign Missionary
    Society of the Protestant Episcopal Church, Forty-Fourth
    through the Seventieth Annual Meetings, 1878 - 1905.
    New York: Various Pub., 1878 - 1905.

Episcopal Church. Journals of the Proceedings of the
    Bishops, Clergy & Laity of the Protestant Episcopal
    Church in the United States Assembled in General
    Convention, 1865-1907. Various Pub., 1865-1907.

Episcopal Church. Diocese of Georgia. Journals of the
    Forty-Third through Fifty-Sixth Annual Conventions of
    the Protestant Episcopal Church in the Diocese of
    Georgia, 1865-1878. Various Pub., 1865-1878.

Episcopal Church. Diocese of Maryland. Journals of the
    Eighty-Second through Ninety-Fifth Annual Conventions of
    the Protestant Episcopal Church in Maryland, 1865-1878.
    Various Pub., 1865-1878.

Episcopal Church. Diocese of North Carolina. Journals of the
    Forty-Ninth through Sixty-Second Annual Conventions of
    the Protestant Episcopal Church in the State of North
    Carolina, 1865-1878. Various Pub., 1865-1878.

Episcopal Church. Diocese of Tennessee. Journals of the
    Proceedings of the Thirty-Third through Sixtieth Annual
    Conventions of the Protestant Episcopal Church in the
    Diocese of Tennessee, 1865-1892. Various Pub.,
    1865-1892.

Episcopal Church. Diocese of Virginia. Journals of the
    Seventieth through Eighty-Third Annual Councils of the
    Protestant Episcopal Church in Virginia, 1865-1878.
    Various Pub., 1865-1878.

Emery, Julia C. A Century of Endeavor, 1821-1921. New York:
    Department of Missions, 1921.

Genovese, Eugene D. Roll, Jordan, Roll. New York: Pantheon
    Books, 1974.

Hayden, Carleton J. "After the War: The Mission and Growth of

the Episcopal Church Among Blacks in the South, 1865-1877." <u>Historical Magazine of the Protestant Episcopal Church</u>, vol. 42 (December 1973): 403-427.

Hopkins, John H. <u>A Scriptural, Ecclesiastical & Historical View of Slavery from the Day of the Patriarch Abraham, to the Nineteenth Century</u>. New York: W.I. Pooley & Co., 1864.

Johnson, Earl. "Crummell and Onderdonk: The Early Admission Policy of the General Theological Seminary Towards Blacks." Unpublished Essay, 1977 (St. Mark's Library of the General Theological Seminary).

Jordan, Winthrop D. <u>White Over Black</u>. New York: W.W. Norton & Co., 1977.

Litwack, Leon. <u>Been in the Storm so Long: The Aftermath of Slavery</u>. New York: Vintage Books, 1980.

Raboteau, Albert J. <u>Slave Religion: The "Invisible Institution" in the Antebellum South</u>. New York: Oxford University Press, 1980.

Reimers, David M. "Negro Bishops and Diocesan Segregation in the Protestant Episcopal Church: 1870-1954." <u>Historical Magazine of the Protestant Episcopal Church</u>, vol. 31 (September 1962): 231-242.

St. Mark's Library of the General Theological Seminary. Bishops of the Episcopal Church Mss.

St. Mark's Library of the General Theological Seminary. Howard Chandler Robbins Collection, Penick Mss.

Smith, H. Shelton. <u>In his Image, but...Racism in Southern Religion, 1780 - 1910</u>. Durham, N.C.: Duke University Press, 1972.

<u>Spirit of Missions</u>. Domestic and Foreign Missionary Society of the Protestant Episcopal Church Church in the United States of America. Edited by the secretaries and general agents, vols. 30 to 72. New York: Various Publishers, 1865 - 1907.

U.S. Congress. House. <u>Report of [Major General] Carl Schurz on the States of South Carolina, Georgia, Alabama, Mississippi, and Louisiana</u>. 39th Cong., 1st sess., 1865.

Ware, John F. W. <u>The Danger of Today</u>. Baltimore, Md.: Cushing & Bailey, 1865.

Wheaton, Nathaniel S. <u>A Discourse on St. Paul's Epistle to Philemon Exhibiting the Duty of Citizens of the Northern States in regard to the Institution of Slavery</u>. Hartford, Conn.: Tiffany & Co., 1851.